PUCK FAIR

A HISTORY

The
History
Press
Ireland

PUCK FAIR

A HISTORY

Seán Moraghan

First published 2013

The History Press Ireland
50 City Quay
Dublin 2
Ireland
www.thehistorypress.ie

British Library Cataloguing in Publication Data.
A catalogue record for this book is available from the British Library.

ISBN 978 1 84588 800 8

Typesetting and origination by The History Press

CONTENTS

Acknowledgements

Many thanks are due to Tommy O'Connor, county librarian, and the staff of the Local History Section at Kerry County Library, Tralee; to the librarian and staff of the Central Library, Grand Parade, Cork; to the librarian and staff of Trinity College Library, Dublin, particularly Martin Whelan who provided a lot of material remotely which otherwise would have been difficult to access; to the Librarian and staff of the National Library of Ireland, Dublin; to the librarian and staff of the Gilbert Library, Dublin; to the keeper and staff of Marsh's Library, Dublin; to the director and staff of the Irish Traditional Music Archive, Dublin.

Among the most useful books of local history, which went towards the creation of the present volume, and which I appreciated greatly, were Kieran Foley's *History of Killorglin*, Patrick Houlihan's *Cast a Laune Shadow*, and Michael Houlihan's *Puck Fair History and Traditions*. Past issues of the *Kerryman* newspaper also formed a wonderful repository of details for Puck Fairs over the years which otherwise would have gone unrecorded.

The following people read and commented helpfully on parts of the draft text: Anne Barrett, Marie Duffy, Cayte Else, Joan Greene, Dr Andrew Kelly, Sinéad Kelly, Kieran McNulty, and Perla Moraghan. Thanks also to Julie Gill, who planted the seed, and to David Grant, who helped me to clarify the picture.

Any errors or omissions remain my own. I remain interested in receiving further historical details to do with the fair, and may be contacted at bonabooks@yahoo.ie.

The Origins of Puck Fair

The Conways

Killorglin's August fair owes its establishment to Jenkin Conway junior, of Killorglin Castle. In 1613, Jenkin sought official permission to hold a fair in the town, and under a patent granted by King James I, dated 10 October, he was granted the right 'to hold a faire in Killorgan on Lammas Day and the day after'.[1] Such grants permitted the holder to collect tolls on every animal sold at the event. Lammas was the name for the Anglican Church's August service, held every 1 August, and fairs held in summer were often granted for that day.

Jenkin's father, also called Jenkin, had been a Welsh settler who was granted Killorglin Castle and the surrounding lands in 1587. Previously, the estate had been a property of the Norman family the Fitzgeralds, Earls of Desmond, who were the lords of north Kerry. Between 1579 and 1583, Gerald Fitzgerald, members of his extended family, and other allies, engaged in a long and bloody rebellion against the imposition of central government control over their extensive territories. In the aftermath the Desmond lands were seized by the Crown, and, under the scheme of the Munster Plantation, they were then rented to English and Welsh members of the nobility, country gentlemen, merchants and soldiers. All the grantees were expected to plant their new estates with further settlers as tenants.

Conway senior had been a captain in Queen Elizabeth I's army during the Desmond Rebellion. He may have had a hand in attacking Killorglin

Castle, and he seems thereafter to have been given the temporary custody of it, along with a garrison of soldiers. He subsequently requested that the lands and castle be bestowed upon him under the terms of the plantation.

The castle had been damaged during the war, and Conway was instructed to build a new castle as part of his grant, with a large 'bawn', or boundary wall.[2] He named the new building Castle Conway, by which name it, and the town of Killorglin, sometimes continued to be known – doing so was typical of a fashion by planters for naming Irish castles or towns after themselves.

Conway's grant was confirmed in 1592, and he was subsequently asked to build houses for eight families. He brought over three of his brothers,[3] and these may have formed some of the quota. He married and had Jenkin, along with two daughters.

The Lammas Fair

It has been suggested that Jenkin senior died in October 1612.[4] After taking over, perhaps Jenkin junior felt that a fair needed to be established in Killorglin as a way of developing the estate, and applied for the patent to hold one.

The first fair was held in August 1614. If the fair thrived under the Conways, we have no account of it, nor whether the native Irish participated in it. Afterwards, the fair was retained as a valuable revenue-gathering asset by the later landlords of Killorglin, the Blennerhassetts, who married into the Conway family around 1662.[5]

The fair itself was held at the top of the hill behind the castle, where the ground levels off into a large triangular space; a shape that was typical of fair fields established during the 1600s in planter communities.[6] The shape can still be recognised on maps of Killorglin town, and today it is defined by Market Road, Mill Road, and Upper Bridge Street/Main Street. The line of Market Road was probably first formed by the boundary wall surrounding Castle Conway. Until modern times this field continued to be used for the display of livestock at the fair.

It is not known when Jenkin junior died, but he and his son Edward were buried within the castle grounds, apparently in a family chapel built there.[7]

Antiquarian Charles Smith saw the tomb and read the inscription upon it sometime during the 1750s. Since then, all trace of this structure has vanished and only part of a single wall of the castle remains. Jenkin junior, the founder of Killorglin's August fair, still lies somewhere in the grounds behind the buildings of Lower Bridge Street, unremembered, as crowds throng the streets around him every August.

The fair appears to have continued long after its foundation and it certainly took place during the eighteenth century. The *Gentleman and Citizen's Almanack* for 1734 listed a fair at 'Kilorgland', County Kerry, for 1 August.[8] After the calendar change of 1752, when Britain and Ireland adopted the Gregorian calendar, fairs and markets became transferred eleven days or so from their original dates, and the Killorglin fair became listed for 12 August, unless the day fell on a Sunday in which case it was scheduled for the following day.[9] The fair is known to have taken place in 1786, when the *Dublin Evening Post* reported an assembly there of agrarian agitators, known as Rightboys.[10] At no time was the fair referred to as 'Puck Fair'.

THE FOLEYS, NEW BARONS OF THE FAIR

It is the author's belief that the introduction of the goat parade and display dates from after 1795, and that it came about after local family, the Foleys, bought the right to hold the fair. The author of a letter which appeared in the *Kerry Sentinel* in 1898 said that the first fair with the goat that he could remember was in 1819.[11] In 1837 the first printed reference to the ritual was made, in Samuel Lewis's *Topographical Dictionary of Ireland*; the description of Killorglin referred to 'Puck Fair, at which unbroken Kerry ponies, goats, &c., are sold, and a male goat is sometimes ornamented and paraded about the fair.'[12] A goat display was not remarked upon during the 1700s. Charles Smith did not mention it in his comprehensive study of the county, published in 1756.

Smith toured Kerry in 1751 and in the years beforehand. He visited Killorglin, saw Castle Conway, described the settlement as a village consisting of several houses which looked 'tolerably well for these parts', and he pointed to its location as an important route into the Iveragh Peninsula.

He noted the salmon fishery of the Laune River.[13] Of the fair, or of a goat ceremony, he said nothing. Smith was a tireless researcher; he talked to landlords and common folk alike in his search for information; and both he and the circle of his fellows were particularly attracted to the unusual. Given all of that, it is hard to imagine that he would have not heard about, been told about, or repeated the story of the parade and display of a goat. A fair he may have ignored, but not a goat ceremony.

In the summer of 1758, Englishman Richard Pococke, Anglican Bishop of Ossory, toured the south of Ireland, including Kerry, and visited Killorglin. On 21 August he wrote a letter detailing his most recent journeys, mentioning that he had crossed the Laune by boat to see the town, and that one of the Blennerhassetts lived there; but, like Smith, he made no mention of the fair or of a goat display.[14]

The custom may have been introduced some time after 1795, when Harman Blennerhassett (1764–1831) decided to sell off his Killorglin mansion and lands. He was a cultured, learned gentleman, who had studied at Trinity College Dublin and had trained as a lawyer. However, in 1793 he had joined the United Irishmen, a secret organisation dedicated to the overthrow of British rule. Even more problematically, he also wished to marry his young niece, Margaret Agnew (b.1779). Both of these factors encouraged him to dispose of his estate and emmigrate to America. He sold his estate to the 1st Baron Ventry, Thomas Mullins (1736–1824), of Burnham, Dingle, to whom the Blennerhassetts were related through marriage. Mullins did not reside at his Killorglin purchase, and the old Blennerhassett house was allowed to gradually fall into disrepair.

Landlords possessed several other property rights, which they could use to gain revenue, sell off, or rent to others for a fee. Harman had possessed not only the mansion and lands but also several other benefits, including the right to hold the August fair. Such subsidiary benefits appear to have been disposed of after he left. In 1797, Thomas Mullins purchased from the Blennerhassetts the right to hold a manorial court, a court for the recovery of debts within Killorglin parish, an old right that had first been granted to Jenkin Conway senior.[15] Mullins also appears to have bought the right of collecting some of the tithes – monies due from tenant farmers to the Church of Ireland. His descendant, the 3rd Baron Ventry, leased the right to these monies to two other individuals in 1834.[16]

The Foleys (originally strong farmers of Anglont, 3km from Killorglin), also benefited from the disposal of Harman's assets. In 1994, Valerie Bary reported that the Foleys had been at Anglont for nine generations, while the family of 'O'Fowlue' was listed in the Killorglin area in a census of Ireland carried out in 1659. 'Sometime around the last quarter of the eighteenth century, it appears that the Foleys became freeholders – unusual at that time', Bary wrote.[17] She believed that the family had bought out their land from MacCarthy of Dungeel, a Catholic landowner who had avoided the land confiscations that had befallen his peers, but who had fallen into debt and had to sell off his estate. The Foleys built an impressive house at Anglont, a large Georgian building which still stands and remains in the family.

In 1798 they bought the fishing rights to the Carha River from Richard Blennerhassett.[18] The Foleys were strongly allied to the Blennerhassetts: Michael James Foley (1783–1867)[19] also known as 'Big Mick', campaigned successfully for candidate Arthur Blennerhassett (1799–1843) of Ballyseedy, Tralee, in the 1837 general election. At some point, around 1800, they appear to have also purchased from the Blennerhassetts the right to hold the fair. One of the Foley men was then entitled to style himself the Baron of the Fair, with the privilege of levying the tolls at the event: the first of these may have been Michael himself, who was certainly called by the title.[20]

THE GOAT PARADE AND DISPLAY

In 1837, Lewis's *Topographical Dictionary of Ireland* indicated that the goat was at first simply paraded around Killorglin. From 1841 it was displayed from a height.[21] In the years afterwards, the goat was raised upon the battlements of the old Conway/Blennerhasset mansion which was no longer occupied by the landlords, and the last tenant of which, Father James Louney (or Luony), had died in 1844. Reports from the mid-1800s indicate that the goat was ornamented with coloured ribbons and this simple decoration is likely to have taken place from the beginning years of the display.[22] By 1870, the castle structure had deteriorated so much that the goat was mounted instead upon a tall wooden platform in the town; this was the precursor of the goat stand used today.

THE GOAT AS MASCOT

All of this suggests that the goat may have been a sort of mascot, a figure-head, or a symbol for the fair. An account of the event, by the *Cork Examiner* in 1846,[23] described the goat as being decorated with gingerbread and salmon, both products that were offered for sale at the event,[24] reinforcing suspicions that the goat display and decoration were intended as emblems of the fair. The use of an animal as a mascot was not a unique one; the fair at Greencastle, County Down, featured a ram placed on the castle walls, and historian of Irish fairs Patrick Logan heard of a custom of decorating the rams at the fair of Dungarvan, County Waterford.[25] More significantly, at Mullinavat, County Kilkenny, a fair used to be held which was also called 'Puck Fair': 'he-goats decorated with ribbons were brought to the fair, the best one amongst them was chosen and set up on a cart, drawn through the fair and set up on high in a field in which the fair was held and the owner of which collected tolls'.[26]

Alternatively, if it was not a mascot for the fair it may have been a mascot for the Foleys themselves, or rather for their faction. The Foleys, in particular 'Big Mick' Foley, were famous faction fighters, leading bands of men into street fights with others.[27] A puck goat would seem to be a suitable symbol for such aggressive activity, as goats are traditionally associated with butting and kicking. If the origin of the goat display lay in the tradition of faction fighting, once that practice was successfully suppressed it may no longer have seemed savoury to refer to it, and different explanations for the origin of the goat display may have been offered instead.

It is impossible to assert with absolute confidence what the origin of the goat ceremony was. It may have had a much older source as a folk custom, which was unique to Killorglin, the nature of which remains unknown or unknowable. A wide range of different stories have been advanced over the years to account for the ceremony, some of which are more believable than others, and these are listed in the appendices at the end of this book.

Notes
1   Richard Hayward, *In The Kingdom of Kerry* (Dundalgan Press, Dundalk, 1946) page 230.
2   Valerie Bary, *Houses of Kerry* (Ballinakella Press, County Clare, 1994) page 155.
3   Charles Smith, *The Ancient and Present State of the County of Kerry: A New Reader's Edition* (Bona Books, Killorglin, 2010) page 15.

4   M.J. de C Dodd, 'The Manor and Fishery of Killorglin, Co Kerry', *Journal of the Galway Archaeological and Historical Society*, Vol. 21, 1944-45, page 167.

5   Bill Jehan, 'Blennerhassett Family of Castle Conway, Killorglin and Rossbeigh in Co Kerry', viewed at www.BlennerhassettFamilyTree.com.

6   Patrick J. O'Connor, *Fairs and Markets of Ireland: A Cultural Geography* (Oireacht na Mumhan, Newcastle West, 2003) page 31.

7   Charles Smith, *The Ancient and Present State of the County of Kerry: A New Reader's Edition* (Bona Books, Killorglin, 2010) page 67.

8   Watson, John, *The Gentleman and Citizen's Almanack* (Dublin, 1734) page 74.

9   See *The Gentleman and Citizen's Almanack* for 1764, 1770.

10   Kieran Foley, *History of Killorglin* (1988) page 34.

11   Quoted in Michael Houlihan, *Puck Fair History and Traditions* (Treaty Press, Limerick, 1999) page 89.

12   Samuel Lewis, *A Topographical Dictionary of Ireland* Vol. II (S. Lewis and Co., London, 1837) page 152.

13   Charles Smith, *The Ancient and Present State of the County of Kerry: A New Reader's Edition* (Bona Books, Killorglin, 2010) page 67.

14   Pádraig Ó'Maidín, 'Pococke's Tour of South and Southwest Ireland in 1758', *Cork Historical and Archaeological Society Journal*, LXIV, Jan-Jun 1959 pages 35-36.

15   Samuel Lewis, *A Topographical Dictionary of Ireland* Vol. II (S. Lewis & Co., London, 1837) page 152.

16   Kieran Foley, *History of Killorglin* (1988) page 37.

17   Valerie Bary, *Houses of Kerry* (Ballinakella Press, County Clare, 1994) page 6; *Census of Ireland, 1659* (Stationery office, Dublin, 1939) page 247.

18   'The humble Petition of Michael James Foley, Philip James Foley, and John Maurice Foley, of Anglont, in the county of Kerry, on their own behalf, and others interested in the weir and fishery of Carha, in the county of Kerry', in *House of Commons Papers, Parts 1-2* (HMSO, London, 1845) pages 80-81.

19   'Ireland. Death of Mr Michael James Foley, of Killorglin', *Dorset Chronicle*, 31 January 1867. (Reprinted from the *Kerry Evening Post*.) 'On the 10th instant, at Anglont, the residence of his son, died this remarkable patriarch, at the advanced age of 84 years … so well known in this county as "Big Mick"'.

20   'Puck Fair', *Tralee Chronicle*, 14 August 1857.

21   'Puck Fair', *Kerry Evening Post*, 11 August 1841.

22   'Puck Fair', *Kerry Evening Post*, 11 August 1841; 'Puck Fair', *Tralee Chronicle*, 16 August 1851.

23   'Puck Fair', *Cork Examiner*, 17 August 1846.

24   Lady Gordon, *The Winds of Time* (John Murray, London, 1934) page 125; 'Puck Fair', *Tralee Chronicle*, 17 August 1850.

25   Patrick Logan, *Fair Day: The Story of Irish Fairs and Markets* (Appletree Press, Belfast, 1986) page 20.

26   Máire MacNeill, *The Festival of Lughnasa* (Oxford University Press, 1962) page 292.

27   Kieran Foley, *History of Killorglin* (1988) page 41.

2

Puck Fair during the Nineteenth and Early Twentieth Centuries

For most of the nineteenth century, Puck Fair was held in what was a small, poor village. Most of Killorglin's population consisted of partially employed agricultural labourers, followed by pub keepers and shopkeepers, and craftsmen such as blacksmiths and harness makers. In 1837 there were 163 houses, with a population of 893 people.[1] Access to the

The goat stand, *c.* 1900. (From the Lawrence Collection. Courtesy of the National Library of Ireland)

Market Road, packed with people and animals, *c*. 1900. (From the Lawrence Collection. Courtesy of the National Library of Ireland)

town for patrons and livestock from the far side of the Laune River was via an old bridge, built some time in the second half of the eighteenth century and was described in 1869 as 'a crazy and patched-up, many-arched structure'.[2]

A visitor in 1822 said, 'For dirt and dreariness, Killorglin may vie with any inhabited place in the universe'.[3] The fair provided an opportunity to give the town a makeover: the houses were decorated with evergreens,[4] and, as the Killorglin correspondent of the *Tralee Chronicle* observed in 1863:

> For some days previous in our good town, for our great annual 'Blow-out' Killorglin threw off its sombre look, and assumed a very pale face, by reason of the application of the seldom-used white-wash brush. Carrying out the old aphorism … 'Were it not for Christmas and Puck Fair, Killorglin would rot.'[5]

The town began to develop from the second half of the nineteenth century. The Ventry Arms Hotel was established from 1865.[6] It stood at the top of Lower Bridge Street, opposite the entrance to Market Road (the building is now Mulvihill's Chemist). A branch of the National Bank of Ireland was established in Killorglin by 1874, which assisted the commercial side of the fair.[7] The old Laune Bridge was acknowledged to be unsafe and a new bridge was completed in 1885, which is the structure still seen today. Most importantly, the Farranfore to Killorglin railway line was opened by the Great Southern and Western Railway Company in January 1885. It entered the town across a viaduct situated towards the seaward side of the town, and the station lay near the present Fexco building on Iveragh Road. The line was later extended west to Valentia Island in 1893, allowing visitors to travel from the town of Cahersiveen. The railway represented a vital improvement to the town, and to the fair. Regular trains were supplemented by special services, which brought visitors in and transported sold animal stock out. (In 1912, it was reported that between 5,000 and 6,000 people arrived and departed by train during the days of the fair, while in the following year a remarkable 200 wagons of stock were despatched.)[8] A second hotel, the Railway Hotel, situated opposite the station, was opened in 1887.

THE DAYS OF THE FAIR

Although the fair is familiar to modern visitors as a three-day event, for most of the nineteenth century it appears to have consisted of two days, 11 and 12 August – the *Freeman's Journal* listed the fair for these two days in 1840.[9]

It later came to be held over three days, starting on the 10 August. This may have arisen for two reasons. It may have been that, as the fame of the fair spread, farmers from further afield brought animals along the roads from greater and greater distances, and a Gathering Day, as it came to be called, gave them time to make the journey for the following day of sale. The 10 August also happened to be the feast day of St Lawrence, for whom the church of Killorglin may have been named (Cill Lorcain, the Church of Lawrence). A church is known to have existed there from at least since 1215, although its precise location is unclear. The 10 August was the day of the patron saint, or the 'pattern day', and it brought people into the town for religious devotions. The two events may have coincided; so much so that Puck Fair was later termed as a fair and a pattern.[10]

Fair Day was always the 11 August, even though buying and selling also took place, although to a lesser extent, on the other two days. Pigs and horses generally seem to have been disposed of by this day, with cattle being sold on 11 August. Scattering Day, the following day, was more for sightseers, for children and young adults, and one less for business than for entertainment.[11] These names for the days do not appear in press reports until the late 1890s.

Occasionally, when the fair day proper fell on a Sunday, the event was extended, beginning a day earlier or, more usually, finishing a day later. Generally, no business was done on the holy day.

THE ORGANISERS

The general organisers of the business aspects of the fair were the Foley family. Michael 'Big Mick' Foley was noted as the Baron of the Fair in 1857, the Baron being the officer who benefited from the tolls and who organised men to see that they were collected.[12] The family more than likely sponsored the bellman, or town crier, who announced important sales and conveyed information to the public; such an official was observed in this duty in 1912.[13] As stated earlier, it is the author's belief that the Foleys also initiated or encouraged the goat parade and display, and this continued to be done in association with the young men of the town; in 1857, 'The young blood of Killorglin did not neglect to elevate the "Puck Goat"', and in 1861, 'The young blood of Killorglin did not forget the time-honoured picture of elevating high above the crowd, and in the most prominent place in our good town, a formidable he-goat'.[14]

From 1908 until approximately 1919 the presentation of the goat was organised by the members of the Killorglin branch of the Total Abstinence Society. The temperance society had been formed in Cork in 1838 by Father Theobald Mathew, and was committed to eliminating alcohol consumption in Ireland, chiefly by administering The Pledge, a personal commitment to abstain from alcohol for life, to thousands of Irish people at monster gatherings throughout the country. Alcohol was the refuge of the poor and quite often led to public drunkenness, fights and domestic abuse, as well as inflaming episodes of violent political action against the police or agents of the landlords.

From the early 1900s the goats were supplied for the event by Michael Houlihan (1878–1968) who also erected the wooden platform and hoisted the goat up for display.[15]

POLICE

The Royal Irish Constabulary (RIC) policed the fair, and would usually draft in other officers from surrounding areas to assist them. There would often be approximately fifty men marshalling crowds that could reach thousands in number.[16] A police station was situated at Killorglin since at least the late 1830s.[17]

At the fair of 1862:

> As Mr Christopher Harold, of Lissataggle,[18] was standing in the very centre of the fair, at about one o'clock, talking to Mr Jonathan Walpole, of Clydane,[19] an athletic young man crept up behind him, and, without the slightest warning, gave him a desperate blow of a heavy iron loaded blackthorn stick on the side of the head. Mr Walpole at once, with great presence of mind, pursued the intended murderer, and laid hold of him, and a policeman coming up promptly he was at once secured and conveyed to the police barracks. The constable got possession of the murderous weapon used on the occasion, which was marked with blood.[20]

After having been attacked on fair day, Mr Harold was again confronted five days afterwards, when a farm labourer who had worked for him threatened him with a pike.[21] It was supposed that Mr Harold's father had 'rendered himself obnoxious to the Roman Catholic clergy of his neighbourhood by holding prayer meetings in his house and rearing in the Protestant faith two children, offsprings of a mixed marriage, intrusted to his care by a deceased friend'.[22]

Along with these random acts of crime, the police had plenty to deal with during the fair, from such common assaults to public drunkenness, faction fighting and Traveller rows.

FARMERS AND THE VARIETY OF ANIMALS SOLD AT THE FAIR

The fair was principally attended by tenant farmers looking to buy or sell livestock. In the 1800s, most farms in Kerry were small, with over 75 per cent of them comprising less than fifteen acres.[23] The small farmers of Kerry, as everywhere in Ireland, rented their land from landlords or their agents, at rates that often proved difficult for many to meet.

Selling pigs, 1954. (Inge Morath ©The Inge Morath Foundation. Courtesy of Magnum Photos)

Farmers travelled with their cattle, horses, sheep and pigs, from a large hinterland around Killorglin, from places such as Glenbeigh, Milltown, and the Dingle Peninsula. In the days before motor transport they rose early in the morning and walked their animals along the roads, often with the aid of a young boy of the family.

Puck Fair was a mixed fair, selling a range of animals: cattle, horses, ponies, sheep, pigs, and goats were offered for sale, but cattle and horses were the biggest attractions. The animals were displayed at the fair field, but buying and selling would also stretch out into Market Road or the other streets of the town. Tolls on animal sales had to be paid to the Foleys, and at one time these were col-lected at the toll house – a stand situated in the middle of the field, which was built some time after 1854; it can be seen on a map of Killorglin from 1894.[24]

Cattle were the single great stock animals of Kerry farms. Using the land for tillage was ignored in favour of grazing cattle, which could be sold at fairs and markets in order to raise much-needed cash to pay rents. Private sales could be small, one or two animals at a time, sometimes to the local butchering trade.[25] Visiting cattle dealers, known as 'jobbers', bought larger numbers, often up to 200 animals a time.[26] Dealers regularly bought animals for further fattening on the rich grasslands of Meath and Kildare, and subse-quent export to Britain from Dublin and other east-coast ports.

Cattle sold at Puck included Kerry Cows, the small, black local breed of south Kerry;[27] these were particularly hardy animals, which could survive on mountain pastureland.

Lady Edith Gordon, of Caragh Lake, wrote of an interaction she had seen at Puck between a farmer and a jobber from Limerick at a fair held during the years of the First World War:

'A hundred quid, Mr Doyle', he suggested, with a spit and an air of having, if anything, exceeded the limits of speculative generosity.

'A hundred and fifty', spiritedly replied the owner of the bullocks.

'Come now, be raysonable; everything is on the down-line'.

'The down-line, is it? I tell you, Mr Quin, prices is killing me. Four pounds an acre I'm after offering for the grazing of a hundred acres, four hundred pounds a year, and I didn't get it at that'.

'And you never expected you would', replied Mr Quin. 'One hundred quid I'm offering you for them bullocks'.

'Ye'd ruin me'.

'I'm ruined meself', replied Mr Quin, ostentatiously producing a large roll of notes, which he proceeded to count between a well-moistened finger and thumb.

'Come now, you'll get no better offer. There's no buyers at the fair at all', he remarked untruthfully, replacing the notes in an inner pocket.

Mr Doyle, with an assumption of utter indifference, surveyed the leaden skies.

'Is that young fellow your son?' he inquired absentmindedly, after a pause, indicating a small boy standing beside Mr Quin, sucking bull's-eyes.

'He is. I'm learning him jobbing'.

'Ye'll be learning him to tell a lot of lies, I'm thinking'.

'I'm not learning him lies at all, Mr Doyle'.

'He'll have a damn bad chance as a jobber so', remarked Mr Doyle, preparing to move on.

'And the hundred quid I'm after offering you?' inquired Mr Quin, anxiously watching Mr Doyle's preparations for departure.

'Ah, don't be talking', said Mr Doyle.

'Well, will we make it a draw?'

'Don't be delusionizing yourself, Mr Quin, it will be no draw', firmly replied Mr Doyle, pushing his way through the crowd in search of a buyer less 'stiff' than Mr Quin.[28]

Horses were important to the event, so much so that one writer called Puck Fair, 'the "Ballinasloe" of Kerry',[29] after the celebrated horse fair held in County Galway. In 1883, the number of horses for sale was reported to be enormous.[30] Generally the animals were shown-off by being trotted along the road, the seller running alongside holding the reins, or by buyers and sellers riding animals at speed. This sometimes led to accidents, particularly as riders might often be drunk.[31] J.M. Synge, playwright of the Irish Literary Revival, visited west Kerry in 1904, staying at Mountain Stage, Glenbeigh, with a family named Harris.[32] He went to see the fair, where one of the first sights to greet him was a small crowd, which had just carried into the church 'a man who had been killed or badly wounded by a fall from a horse'.[33] As reported by the *Kerry Sentinel*:

> It would seem that amongst the large number of persons exhibiting their horses and galloping them 'for their wind' was a small farmer named Tangney from the Scartaglin district, and in the act of doing so galloped right bang and at a terrible speed into another horse which was being run against him at as high a velocity. The result of the collision was that the horse ridden by Tangney had its spinal column broken and fell dead on the ground that second. As a consequence of the fearful compact poor Tangney was dashed to the ground with terrific force, and, though not killed, it is feared that his chances of recovery are but very slender.[34]

The animals offered up for sale were generally of three classes. The best were 'hunters', horses suitable for fox hunting and other cross-country pursuits. These were sought out by local gentlemen or members of the clergy, while some buyers travelled from other parts of the country, even some from England, to find these quality animals. The second class consisted of horses suitable for pulling cabs in service in the towns, or the carriages that travelled between them.[35] The third kind were for agricultural use, animals of no remarkable breeding but strong enough to pull ploughs in the fields and carts along the road, 'a good, serviceable farmer's horse'.[36]

The Fair Field, *c.* 1900. (From the Lawrence Collection. Courtesy of the National Library of Ireland)

The proportion of good-quality horses offered at Puck was small. In 1888, 'very few good class animals were offered for sale', so that buyers were in turn sometimes offered money for a good horse which they had just purchased.[37] In 1873, the *Tralee Chronicle* reported that:

> ... well-bred colts were bought at first-class prices ... [several buyers] especially those from England, complained of the inferior breed of horses offered for sale as not suiting their purposes. Hunters, which were remarkably scarce, were eagerly looked for, and brought good prices. Lord Dunraven[38] was amongst those in market trying for hunters, but could not get any to suit him. The principal description of horses offered for sale were two and three year olds. They were of a rather clumsy class, and chiefly suited for agricultural purposes.[39]

Kerry Ponies, also called Kerry Bog Ponies, were noted as being characteristic of the fair. In 1825 a report by the *Freeman's Journal* of 'the fair of Killorglin' noted that 'Handsome ponies (for which that part of the country was formerly so remarkable), in particular, bore an unprecedented price.'[40] These were a local breed of small, hardy animals which lived wild on the mountains and bog land of Kerry. 'Numbers of them are brought down from the mountains to Killorglin fair, in droves of perhaps a score[41] together, not one of them having been ever embarrassed by a halter[42], till sold there', observed the *Topographical Dictionary of Ireland*.[43] They were particularly agile animals, well suited to bog ground or wet conditions, and were used as farm workhorses, often carrying loads of turf. The breed was said to be descended from another Irish breed, the Irish Hobby, but a descent from the Asturian pony of northern Spain was also suggested.

Their quantity and quality were said to have declined over time. In 1837, the *Topographical Dictionary of Ireland* noted that 'The Kerry ponies, once so famed, and originally of Spanish or rather Moorish extraction, were formerly strong enough for farming purposes, but now, by injudicious cross-ing, are so degenerated as to be fit only for the saddle and for very light weights.'[44] A decline in their numbers was feared in 1873: 'There were not as many Kerry ponies as last year – indeed it is to be feared that this pretty and prized race is dwindling away every year.'[45] (During the twentieth century, the breed was thought to have finally died out, but was rescued from extinc-tion during the 1990s.) A comparative idea of their value in relation to horses can be gained from their selling prices: in 1878, mountain ponies sold for £5, while horses sold for between £30 and £70.[46]

Dragging horses down Lower Bridge Street, 1984. (© David Hurn. Courtesy of Magnum Photos)

Of course, goats were sold at the fair. Puck goats were offered for sale in 1850,[47] while in 1856 some dealers 'picked up lots of goats: 20 or more might be seen in several droves'.[48] They were important farm animals in Ireland during the nineteenth century; they were 'the poor man's cow'.[49] They needed less land to roam than cows and thrived on poor or mountain land, while providing milk and meat. They were considered, along with the Kerry Ponies, to be the animals that really typified the event. Indeed, so important were they that it was their presence – rather than the goat on the stage – that was said to have given rise to the very name of Puck Fair.[50] The animals were driven to the fair as late as 1913,[51] but they were no longer mentioned in press reports after that date, although, in the 1920s, they remained on a list of animals for which a toll had to be paid.[52]

Pigs were always offered for sale but do not seem to have been in big demand until the 1890s.[53] They were always traded on Gathering Day. In 1895, the largest pig fair ever known in Killorglin took place, with brisk demand from buyers from Limerick, as well as from Cork and Tralee – 1,800 pigs were sold and carried away by train. In 1907, all the pigs offered for sale were quickly bought up, packed into train wagons and despatched before the afternoon had begun.

Servant Boys and Girls

During springtime, young men and women who had been hired out as farm workers and domestic servants would travel back to Puck.[54] In 1898, the *Kerry Sentinel* commented: 'As our readers know there is not a "servant boy or servant girl" within a radius of 10 miles of "Puck" who does not insist, when making a bargain with an employer, to be allowed to go to Killorglin for "Puck" fair'.[55] Workers also returned from seasons at the more prosperous farms around Tralee and north Kerry.[56]

They would arrive at the fair wearing their best Sunday clothes. They were looking for excitement, to meet each other, or to have a 'match' – an agreement to marry, and the dowry required, arranged by their parents. 'The number of "matches" made between young couples is not stated, but was probably beyond the average', surmised a correspondent of the *Kerry Sentinel* in 1899. Lady Edith Gordon later observed:

The bargaining for husbands and wives is done by the parents on market or fair days, and, over the inevitable glass of whisky, the future of the rising generation is arranged. The young people themselves, though never coerced if really unwilling, are seldom consulted … often a match will fall through owing to the parents of the 'boy' refusing to part with an extra heifer, or those of the girl holding on to a few pounds: a 'fortune' taking, as a rule, the form of a mixed amount of cash and cattle. The extraordinary part of the bargain is that a girl never gets the benefit of her own fortune, which is invariably used as a dowry for the brothers and sisters of the bridegroom.[57]

GENTLEMEN OF THE COUNTY

The landed gentlemen of Kerry went to Puck, mostly just looking for good horses on the fair day itself. 'The "kid glove" gentlemen of the county were pretty fairly represented at the fair,' wrote the *Tralee Chronicle* in 1877, 'but that class of the community took up their quarters at some of the beautiful villas adjacent to the town and kept away from the noise and bustle.'[58] In 1883 it was reported that a nephew of the Duke of Leinster bought the puck goat that had been displayed, for the sum of £1.[59]

MILITIA

Recruiters from the Kerry Militia also attended. Each county in Ireland had a reserve force of soldiers which existed to suppress episodes of rural violence. Generally, the men were Catholics while their officers were Protestants, with the highest ranks often held by members of the aristocracy. In 1857, three Staff Sergeants, accompanied by Captain Spring and Staff Surgeon Dr Thomas Maybury, roamed through the fair and enrolled about half a dozen volunteers.[60]

SIGHTSEERS AND HOLIDAY MAKERS

Puck Fair was an attraction not just for those with business to do; thousands attended purely for entertainment purposes. Many of these visitors came from the broad hinterland around Killorglin, from Tralee, and from counties Cork, Limerick and Clare.[61] J.M. Synge observed, 'Here there were a number of people who had come in for amusement only, and were walking up and down, looking at each other – a crowd is as exciting as champagne to these lonely people, who live in long glens among the mountains – and meeting with cousins and friends.'[62] At the fair of 1909, *The Kerryman* reported:

> During the night, instead of retiring to their slumbers, a good many remained pacing through the streets, or at some of the games which were in progress, until morning, with no other than the light from a few candles, and which were well patronised until then. The square, indeed, with the light from the platform and that from the several tables and games, looked like a huge stall in a bazaar or something of that kind, and the streets presented an extraordinary appearance, having some of the houses opened and illuminated and others in slumbering darkness.[63]

Visiting an agricultural fair, of course, carried some inconveniences for the general public: 'In consequence of the continual downpour the fair field and the streets of the town were covered with mud, thereby rendering the occasion most uncomfortable to pedestrians. And nevertheless, very many of the young ladies wore petticoats which rivalled the driven snow at starting, but alas were not much improved by being worn at "Puck".'[64]

During the 1800s, almost all of the sightseers were Irish. Foreign tourists did not start to take in the fair in large numbers until after the Second World War, but some were noted as early as 1912: 'There is reason to know that ladies and gentlemen from England, America, and even so far away as strange Japan, when touring at Killarney, Caragh Lake, and other neighbouring places, motor to Killorglin to see the strange sight of a fair presided over by a puck goat'.[65]

THE TRAVELLERS

The most significant group to attend the fair beyond the farming community were the Travellers – whom the settled community called 'Tinkers', due to their trade of repairing tin pots and pans. Puck Fair seems to have been the most

Traveller caravans parked along the Killarney Road, 1954. (Inge Morath © The Inge Morath Foundation. Courtesy of Magnum Photos)

important event in their calendar; during a row between two sets of Travellers at the fair of 1908, one of the men from one side shouted at the other, 'We were at Puck Fair since the year before the Flood, and in spite of ye we'll be there the year before the day of General Judgement'.[66] Beyond buying and selling, it appears to have been an occasion for assemblies and discussions between families.[67]

Most of the Travellers who came to Puck were from Kerry and County Limerick.[68] They travelled throughout Munster in canvas-covered horse-drawn caravans from fair to fair. At Killorglin they invariably parked their caravans in a line along the far bank of the Laune River – from the bridge, stretching back along the Killarney road. They usually arrived a week or two before the fair and spread out about the local area, the men seeking work repairing household items.[69] Sometimes they pitched up early at Douglas, about two and a half miles east of Killorglin, near the shores of Castlemaine Bay. (After Puck Fair, the Travellers went on to other August fairs, such as Kenmare and Bantry.)[70]

Their other great trade was selling horses, although the animals were not thought by the wider community to be of good quality, having been bred without attention to features that it might have been useful to encourage or discourage. They were often sold between the Travellers themselves, or as often simply swapped, without any cash transaction.[71]

Traveller children and a traditional caravan, 1954. (Inge Morath © The Inge Morath Foundation. Courtesy of Magnum Photos)

Along with selling horses went the sport of racing them against each other, usually from Chapel Cross in the town to one of the quays along the seaward end of the Laune River. One such occasion was watched by a Killorglin correspondent for the *Tralee Chronicle* in 1847:

> Dull and spiritless we passed the earlier part of the day, until, about one o'clock, a rush in the direction of the Chapel, the old racing ground, assured us that Mr Wallace, the celebrated Limerick Tinker, with his companions, each mounted on a nag ... had made his appearance. Then were the preliminaries of the usual race, justly and fairly arranged by 'Father Wallace'. The wager was laid – a 'quart and sweepstakes'.[72] Eight Rosinantes[73] entered the lists, off they flew, a mile-heat, now they ascend the hill, at one moment Jimmy Ryan leads – at the next the redoubtable and venerable Wallace is seen in advance, urging on his 'fair mare Meg' to her fleetest speed. He leads the van,[74] until within two 'lengths' of the winning post, Meg exhausted, and bleeding profusely, from the too cruel and repeated application of whip and spur, fell, as we thought, to rise no more. Jimmy Ryan was triumphant, but the venerable Wallace, in the fury of disappointment, rushed at the victor and tore him from the noble animal he bestrode.[75]

In 1850, 'The "travelling tinkers" were as usual in force swopping nags, and riding races'.

> In one of those races a poor countryman was nearly killed – having come in contact with the running horses, he was thrown down and trampled and crushed. It was first supposed that he was killed, but after a long time he came to and was able to go home in a very weak state.[76]

While the men were selling horses or racing, the women sang ballads in the streets. Some reports claimed that Traveller women wandered through the fair as pickpockets.[77]

Generally, the settled community of Killorglin had an ambivalent attitude towards the Travellers. For some, their bouts of drinking were not welcomed; 'Then comes the finale, an adjournment to some village hostelerie to break the landlord's glasses and each others heads, as an absolutely necessary wind up', wrote the Killorglin correspondent of the *Tralee Chronicle* in 1861. Yet for others among the public, fistfights among the Travellers were sometimes sought out as a kind of free street entertainment. A big fight took place on the fair day of 1908:

> Talk of the tinkers from Puck, but my goodness, if you saw the row on Tuesday evening! Sheridans v Coffeys and Foleys (tinkers)[78] you would at least think that we wouldn't have one spared for next year. A regular 'life-in-their-fist' row it seemed for a while, but after about half-an-hour … the RIC succeeded in restoring quietness, when the merits of Limerick and Kerry were well threshed out, and 'Up Kerry' was ringing through the air even above the other shouts. It is hard to say which side had the better as they didn't fight to a finish – perhaps they left that for Kenmare[79] on Saturday: but such a fight couldn't be seen again … If this be finished in Kenmare we hope our friends there will let us know the result as we're most interested.[80]

A Killorglin correspondent wrote of the fair of 1909:

> Some people are still regretting that a greater number of the tinkers didn't make their appearance, as they say that these Irish Gypsies are characteristic of the Fair, and these very same people even go as far as saying that they are sorry they didn't see a few good free fights, as I suppose they would also say this is characteristic of the fair as well. It wouldn't be so bad to have these visitors come to Puck, but the big trouble would be to get them out afterwards. In fact the few who did come have not made their exit up to the present,[81] though we expected they'd go to Milltown Sports[82] and not return.[83]

Kerry Travellers, the Coffey family, were important participants in these fights. Walter Starkie, later a renowned scholar of the Romany gypsies, was as a child brought along to the fair of 1904:

> While we were talking I heard shouts coming from the bar, and the sound of broken bottles and glasses. 'The Coffeys are beginning as usual to raise hell in there', said Shamus. 'I must be off with the boys', said Joe, hobbling into the public house rapidly. 'Joe is a Coffey, so he must join in the fun,' said Shamus, 'every Puck Fair it is customary for the tinkers of the Coffey tribe to run a-mock in Killorglin. It is their ancient privilege, and if you'd wait until the evening after the goat procession starts you'd see the peelers[84]

drivin' them tinkers out of the town. An' they'll all go out together in their carts with their women and their donkeys and their pots and pans, and they'll raise their fists and bawl out blisterin' curses at the town.' [85]

A famous row, later called the Battle of Killorglin, was recalled by an old man in conversation with a journalist from *The Irish Times* in 1931:

The tinkers of Kerry are a distinct race. There was the famous Black Moll, one of the queens of the tribe, and the Caseys … On Gatherin' Day a large army of tinkers from other counties arrived, prepared to make their fortunes at Puck, but the Killorglin tinkers, hearing of the invasion, met their rivals on the bridge coming from Killarney, and 'scathered' them before the fair began. The tale is told in Kerry as a great feat. 'They were routed', an old man told me, 'for thinkin' they could camp at Puck Fair, when the Caseys and Black Moll regarded the territory as their property.' [86]

MUSICIANS, SINGERS AND BANDS

Many musicians and ballad singers played and sang at Puck Fair. At the fair of 1913 it was noted that there were, 'Fiddlers, accordeon-players, wandering minstrels of all ages, several being foreigners.[87] It is compulsory on the instrumentalists to play lively music, the "madder the measure" the better chance of a reward, but a tender melody may now and then be accepted; but the singer may sing his strains to the wind unless his are songs of sadness.'[88]

Many of these musicians were Travellers. At the fair of 1875:

all the itinerant music 'tribe' from the shrill 'penny-whistler' to the buzzing piper, were numerously represented, and their playing seemed to please their respective open-mouthed audiences so much that when the musician wished to 'wet his whistle' or 'take round the cap' some members of his audience would volunteer his services and do both for him.[89]

Ballad singers were often Traveller women, and two songs from their repertoire were mentioned in 1862: 'The Ballad of Bull's Run', and 'The Tinware Lass'. The first was an American Civil War song composed in New York, only a year

Young musicians, 1954. (Inge Morath ©The Inge Morath Foundation. Courtesy of Magnum Photos)

before, praising the Union forces of the 69th Irish Regiment, particularly their leader, Captain Thomas Francis Meagher, who had fought bravely against greater numbers of Confederate forces at Bull Run, Virginia. The ballad was quickly transmitted from Irish-America back to Ireland. 'The Tinware Lass', on the other hand, was a song that had been known in Ireland since the 1820s:

> One evening not very long ago,
> Being in the spring time of the year,
> With crimson cloak and rosy cheeks
> This fair maid stepped forth with her ware
> I thought that she no mortal was,
> Till near me she did advance
> Then I found she was no deity,
> But a charming handsome tinware lass.[90]

In 1904, at the foot of the platform where the goat was placed upon a stage, J.M. Synge heard a young ballad-singer, John Purcell, 'howling a ballad in honour of Puck', which he also had printed for sale on slips of green paper:

All young lovers that are fond of sporting, pay attention for a while,
I will sing you the praises of Puck Fair, and I'm sure it will make you smile;
Where the lads and lassies coming gaily to Killorglin can be seen,
To view the Puck upon the stage, as our hero dressed in green.

And hurra for the gallant Puck so gay,
For he is a splendid one:
Wind and rain don't touch his tail,
For his hair is thirty inches long.

Across the Square, he saw a man and a woman sing the alternating verses of another ballad, about the Russian and Japanese War.[91] The woman sang the verse below, after which they both sang a concluding line:

Now the Russians are powerful on sea and on land;
But the Japs they are active, they will them command,
Before this war is finished I have one word to say,

There will be more shot and drowned than in the Crimea.[92]

Travelling musicians, 1955. (© The Kennelly Archive)

He came upon a third singer near the fair green: 'As we came out again into the road, an old man was singing an out-spoken ballad on women in the middle of the usual crowd. Just as we passed it came to the scandalous conclusion; and the women scattered in every direction, shrieking with laughter and holding shawls over their mouths'.[93]

During the first decade of the 1900s, bands also played. The boys of the Tralee Industrial School travelled by train to Killorglin and entertained fairgoers with selections of Irish airs on the mornings of the Scattering Days and accompanied the dethronement ceremonies. From 1908 they were replaced by a new brass band formed by the Killorglin branch of the Total Abstinence Society, who played at the fairs until 1920.

Another kind of musical entertainment may have come courtesy of the organ grinders – men who carried machines which played the same tune over and over again while the operator wound a handle. In 1901, they are listed once as among the attractions of the fair.[94] Generally a cup for collecting donations lay on top of the machine, or was held in the operator's free hand. The player wandered through the crowd playing the same tune until he was paid, either in appreciation, or in order to get him to move on.

TRAMPS, BEGGARS AND CHANCERS

There were tramps and beggars, petty thieves and pickpockets at Puck Fair, and at the fair of 1850, the *Tralee Chronicle* reported that, 'Many people were robbed, so that pickpockets must have been in force, and the thronged state of the fair gave them peculiar facilities for plying their callings'.[95]

When Synge walked to the fair he noted:

On the main roads, for many days past, I have been falling in with tramps and trick characters of all kinds, sometimes single and sometimes in parties of four or five.

Just outside the town, near the first public-house, blind beggars were kneeling on the pathway, praying with almost Oriental volubility for the souls of anyone who would throw them a coin.

'May the Holy Immaculate Mother of Jesus Christ,' said one of them, 'intercede for you in the hour of need. Relieve a poor blind creature, and

Stalls and carts surround the goat stand, *c.* 1900. (From the Lawrence Collection. Courtesy of the National Library of Ireland)

may Jesus Christ relieve yourselves in the hour of death. May He have mercy, I'm saying, on your brothers and fathers and sisters for evermore.'[96]

It has been observed that Synge may have been influenced by the language used by the blind beggars at Puck Fair, when he wrote some of the dialogue for the characters Christy Mahon and Shawn Keogh in *The Playboy of the Western World*.[97]

Visitor Robert Lynd met only a single beggar in 1912, who spent the day kneeling on the muddy footpath with a printed sign about his neck with the message 'Pray for the repose of the departed souls of your friends', as he pleaded, 'I ask you for the love of God. Give a penny to a poor stone-blind man and he without sight'.[98] Lynd observed that, 'His was evidently a lucrative profession. I saw a priest stop to put a sixpence in his hand'. It was a custom that was dying out, however, as the man recalled that once five or six blind men like himself would attend the fair.

TRICKSTERS

Puck attracted a group of sharp characters who travelled from fair to fair, intent on making money from the crowds. They were known as 'trickies' or 'thimble-riggers',[99] the latter after the game in which members of the public were invited to locate a pea, seemingly placed by the trickster under one of three thimbles, which were then shuffled about at speed. The thimble-rigger usually had an accomplice among the crowd, who pretended to be unknown to him and who was allowed to win a few times, thus drumming up public interest and excitement. In reality the pea was hidden under the operator's thumb. The English writer William Makepeace Thackeray saw a couple of these characters in action at Killarney races in August 1842:

> A ragged scoundrel … went bustling and shouting through the crowd with his dirty tray and thimble, and as soon as he had taken his post, stated that this was the 'royal game of thimble' and calling upon 'gintlemin' to come forward. And then a ragged fellow would be seen to approach, with as innocent an air as he could assume, and the bystanders might remark that the second ragged fellow almost always won. Nay, he was so benevolent, in many instances, as to point out to various people who had a mind to bet, under which thimble the pea actually was. Meanwhile, the first fellow was sure to be looking away and talking to some one in the crowd; but somehow it generally happened – and how of course I can't tell – that any man who listened to the advice of rascal No.2, lost his money.[100]

The sleight-of-hand gambling game 'Trick o' the Loop' was often played.[101] A leather belt was rolled up tight and a member of the public paid to find the centre of the loop with a long nail, or similar object. But because of the way the belt was wound the trickster was then able to snap it straight without trapping the nail – the loop appeared to have vanished, and the gambler lost his wager. Beforehand, the mark would have been allowed to play for free and win, after which he was invited to bet, and lose.

It is probable that the 'Three Card Trick' was practised at Puck Fair during this period; Thackeray drew a performance of it elsewhere in 1842, and it was generally known from the 1870s, but it is not referred to in connection with the fair until the middle of the following century.

Some of the tricksters were Travellers. In 1912, Robert Lynd met a Traveller at a street corner:

Horseless carts, boxes, and all sorts of things lined the gutter, and this big fellow had found an upturned barrel, on the end of which he spread out the four aces of a pack of cards as a preliminary to a gamble.

The game was to guess which suit would turn up when the pack was cut: he gave you two to one against any suit you liked.

'It's a fair game', he kept saying, as he shuffled the cards. 'It's a fair game. The fairest game in Ireland.'

I said the tinker was irresistible, but the country people who crowded round and looked at the four aces over each other's shoulders apparently did not find him so, for they allowed him to go on shuffling the cards and soothering that it was a fair game, the fairest game in Ireland, without making any move to test it.[102]

STALLS AND DIVERSIONS

While the animal sales went on at the fair field, there was plenty of other buying and selling done on the main streets of the town, by a variety of hawkers and hucksters at stalls and standings. Such traders at other Kerry fairs are known to have had to pay a fee, and it is likely that they had to do the same at Puck Fair, although no record remains; for a survey of tolls and customs levied in Ireland, carried out in 1818, it was reported that at the four fairs of Kilgobnet, owned by Rowland Blennerhassett, hucksters standings on fair day were charged at 4*d*, while at Milltown fair, owned by Sir John Godfrey, hawkers' standings cost 6*d*.[103]

Among the pitches of the 1890s there were carts displaying boots and brogues, while second-hand clothes were auctioned by what were known as 'castclothes men'. Robert Lynd watched a red-haired man from the north of Ireland standing on a platform with a clothes-rail beside him:

He was trying to sell a tweed overcoat which he had slung on his arm, and somebody had just made a low bid for it. The auctioneer listened derisively.

'Seven shillings?' he repeated, with simulated incredulity. 'The shirt you'll wear at your wake will cost more than that. And I hope', he added, with a satirical nod at the bidder, 'I hope the corpse will look better than the patient.'

While the crowd was laughing, he took up a long white waterproof coat and gave it a slap of approval.

'Here's the greatest bargain of the fair', he said. 'If you saw that coat in the window of a draper's shop, you'd see a ticket on it marked one pound seven and sixpence: divil a lie! The drapers, I tell you, are worse robbers than the landlords.'[104]

As often as not, the Puck Fair crowds listened to the various street hawkers as if they were just another kind of entertainment, and had no interest in buying. Lynd concluded: 'Not an offer from the crowd. Just a sea of faces waiting for the next jest and gibe, everybody taking a thorough pleasure in the names that the red man was calling them'.[105] Lady Gordon also observed, about half a dozen years later, that the business and bustle on the streets was often diversion enough for people:

> Up and down the town all day, in the mist and the mud, the buying and bargaining, with intervals for refreshment, continued. In the afternoon, the crowd, reinforced by girls in hats of dazzling smartness, surged beneath the 'Puck', round which, in booths, an enormous trade was being done; each garment displayed being accompanied by facetious remarks from the auctioneer and witty sallies from the onlookers. Every now and then a drove of sheep or a stampeding cow would charge wildly into their midst, scattering women and children; while the news that 'Maggie McKenna's father-in-law had sold his little "harse" to a dealer from Cork' sent a whole cavalcade off with a rush to the green to assist in the completion of the bargain.[106]

There were opportunities for diversion with gambling at a roulette table or a variation of it called the 'Wheel of Fortune'.[107] There were shooting galleries.[108] The game of 'Aunt Sally' (also known as 'Maggies') was played for many years at Puck Fair: a block of wood fashioned like a human face had a hole where the nose should be; this was filled usually by the bowl-end of a smoking-pipe, or by a piece of wood, and players paid to knock these off by throwing objects at a distance in the hope of winning money.[109] In 1912, Robert Lynd watched an old man with a humped back who was running a penny draw:

> He was selling bits of cardboard about half the length of your finger at a penny apiece. You drew one of these at a venture out of a small box he passed round, and on it the name of your prize was written. The old man took the scrap of cardboard from the purchaser and read out the inscription. 'A lady's gold ring', he would announce, and with great solemnity would hand a ring that had once been in a lucky-bag over to the winner.
>
> Or he would read out impressively, 'A pair of gentleman's bootlaces', and would present the prize to the winner, beaming congratulation. It was a lottery in which there were no blanks. The poorest prize I could see was a ballad. I would not call a ballad a poor prize in ordinary circumstances, but this old man did not give his victims ballads in the ordinary form. He had simply cut the ballads … and his prizes were only these clipped snippets.[110]

The range of stalls and the variety of attractions at the fair were recalled after the fair of 1908:

> In order to give you an idea of how the people enjoyed themselves, here's a list of the tables which were fixed at various places, which I could see: – four roulettes …, six dice boards, four penny lotteries, eight fortune-telling birds[111] …, seven rifle shooting ranges, two ring shooting stands, one race horse game, three 'Hairy family' or 'Maggie' firing ranges, about a dozen card playing tables made by turning empty Guinness barrels upside down, and about thirty others [112]

In the 1870s, travelling theatres began to appear, most likely presenting a varied popular programme of serious and comic acting and singing.

> Not alone was the fair ground crammed with buyers and sellers of cattle, but the streets at either side were lined with dealers and gamblers of all sorts, and to add to the business of the day, and to occupy the time of the idlers, there was erected on a field, to the left of the road leading to the

Courthouse, a shedding of some magnitude, which, on enquiry, I learned to be the 'Shamrock Theatre', so called, I presume, from the emblems of nationality emblazoned on the portals of the establishment. This place of amusement was well patronised – the charge for admission being very low – by the boys and girls of the district, who came to the fair dressed in their best with the intention of availing themselves of a general holiday.[113]

The theatres seem to have continued to appear at Puck Fair into the 1890s, with a general account of the fair in 1894 describing:

An itinerant theatre, outside which the clown (with red nose and white face as usual, but otherwise in everyday costume) is beating a drum and announc-ing his programme for one penny, while his prima-donna stands at the door, resplendent in a pink garment, trimmed with gold tinsel embroidery.[114]

From the early 1900s, until the mid-1920s, a family named Tierney provided fairground amusements such as merry-go-rounds.[115] In 1905, a company called O'Farrell and Sons visited the fair, presenting hobby-horse rides, swing-boats and a shooting gallery.[116]

PUCK FOOD

Plenty of food was available during the fair. From the early 1900s, many houses in Killorglin were converted into restaurants, or the women of the houses presented food on tables outside their doors; J.M. Synge saw stalls 'set out with cheap cakes and refreshments, and one could see that many houses had been arranged to supply the crowds who had come in'.[117] In tents set up at the fair field, women sold mutton pies, pork pies and leather cakes (cakes with a caramel or hard butterscotch filling).[118] Fresh salmon from the Laune River was also usually available.[119] Ulsterman Robert Lynd noted dulse for sale (pieces of dried seaweed also known as dillisk) that was eaten as a snack; he would have been familiar with it as a popular offering at Ulster fairs.[120] During the First World War, Lady Gordon saw 'old women with barrows selling dried fish, unripe apples stolen from the neighbouring orchards, gingerbread and bull's-eyes'.[121]

Street drinkers, 1971. (© Josef Koudelka. Courtesy of Magnum Photos)

Drinking at Puck Fair

There were many public houses in Killorglin and, during the fair, large tents were also set up selling beer, including 'flaggons of Beamish and Crawford XX'.[122] In 1864, the local correspondent lamented that these had dwindled in number, but that twenty years before they could be counted by the score. No account of them from Puck Fair survives, but they had been observed at the fair of Cahirmee, County Cork:

> Right along the centre of the fair field there was a line of rectangular tents, each of which exhibited a gaudy sign on the outside, over the entrance, bearing some such legend as this: 'Erin's Pride. Timothy Murphy, licensed to sell Beamish and Crawford's porter'; and well patronised and noisy they seemed to be.[123]

The fair was an occasion when people who otherwise lived in rural isolation got to meet each other, see relatives, and celebrate the sale or purchase of stock. It was a rare opportunity for them to drink – they were now surrounded by temptation and had cash in their pockets; binge drinking was the result. 'There were very many drunken persons about the town,' wrote the *Tralee Chronicle* of the fair of 1850, 'and in the evening a good deal of partial rioting took place, both in the streets and on the roads leading therefrom, particularly towards the mountains.'[124] In 1878, the *Kerry Sentinel* reported that 'a good number seemed to enjoy themselves very well, if one could judge by the large numbers who were, to use a popular phrase, 'half seized over'.'[125] In 1895:

A great number of the drunken and rowdy elements were in evidence, and consequently the railway officials experienced considerable difficulty in performing their duties. It appears that one of the railway porters was assaulted by a man of the farming class, who resides at Glenbeigh, situated about seven miles from Killorglin. Mr Moore, stationmaster, Mr Loughrey, assistant stationmaster, and Mr Doyle, relief clerk, with others of the railway staff, came to the scene with a view to obtaining the aggressor's name, when instantly they were attacked by a crowd of Glenbeighans who waved sticks in all directions.

Then ensued a fearful onslaught on the whole of the railway staff, who acted with admirable pluck. They were quite defenceless against the attack, being without any means to defend themselves. The public cleared off the platform instantly and left the railway people to the mercy of the rioters. Unluckily there was only one policeman (Constable O'Regan) to protect them. Two of the porters and assistant stationmaster were in the thick of the fight, and were all most grievously injured. One of the men is almost in danger of his life, and Mr Loughrey was thrown across the buffers and automatic brakes between the carriages and beaten down with sticks, but came out again to the rescue of the other men.[126]

Another incident, which appears to date from the late 1800s, illustrates the hazards of drinking at Puck Fair:

Mickey Doolan, a Castleisland man, and a friend of his, had attended the opening day of the fair with some cattle. Prices that day were good and the two had little difficulty in disposing of their stock. The evening was long, their pockets were full, and the 'spirits' of the fair were plentiful and cheap.

Suited characters, 1954. (Inge Morath © The Inge Morath Foundation. Courtesy of Magnum Photos)

Mickey and his pal sampled the products of every one of the thirty odd pubs in the town.

Nightfall found them with no place to rest their, by then, weary and unguidable bodies. Mickey, no doubt with some difficulty, managed to focus his eyes on a barrel that was lying on its side near a showman's stall on The Square. Investigation showed it to contain hay used in packing the showman's prizes … They crawled in and collapsed in a sleep of complete exhaustion.

Morning's light started a new day's hilarious gaiety: Mickey and his pal, still unconscious of their surroundings, were discovered by some practical jokers. Their bed was carefully directed into the centre of the street, and a hefty punch sent it careering down The Square … The screams of the two captives, issuing from the rapidly revolving barrel, and the tally-hoing mob in its rear created pandemonium through the length of the fair, that terminated only when the barrel was finally arrested on reaching the Laune Bridge. Mickey, long since passed to his eternal rest, and his pal, emerged shaken and terrified, but, except for a few bruises, were none the worse from their exploit.[127]

Perhaps it was not always the drinkers but the drink that was the problem at Puck Fair. Samuel Hussey, land agent, wrote in 1904 that one Killorglin publican mixed up a special whiskey for the fairs, which consisted of 'A gallon of fresh, fiery whisky. A pint of rum. A pint of methylated spirit.

Two ounces of corrosive sublimate. Three gallons of water.' Methylated spirit was alcohol to which indigestible substances and a coloured dye had previously been added to make it undrinkable; it was used as a fuel or as a cleaning agent. Corrosive sublimate was another name for mercuric chloride, traditionally a remedy for syphilis, and which was highly toxic. No wonder Hussey observed that, 'An Irishman's constitution must be tougher than that of an ostrich to enable him to consume much of the filthy poison'.[128] (Drunkenness was not confined to men: at the fair of 1901 most of the arrests for intoxication were of women.)[129]

After the Total Abstinence Society took over the running of the event, from 1908, it was said that there was a 'considerable decrease in the number who celebrated the event by getting drunk'.[130] The following year, the Killorglin correspondent of the *Kerryman* said that the fair had been the quietest for years, 'as well as being the most sober. I don't think there were a dozen to be got at the whole fair who were what could be called badly drunk.'[131]

Faction Fighting

Faction fighting, a kind of semi-organised battle in which two or more crowds met each other and fought with stones, fists and sticks, or any implement they could find, took place at Irish fairs. 'The sticks used were of different kinds,' wrote Patrick Logan, 'probably the most popular was a heavy blackthorn about 3-4ft long and held about one-third of the way along the shaft so that the near end could be used to protect the elbow'.[132] Other sticks were made of a heavy ash sapling. Sticks were often seasoned to make them harder, or fashioned at the top with a lump of lead or iron to make them even more devastating as weapons. Blows from the sticks often badly injured and sometimes killed participants. Most of those involved tended to be men, although some women took part too. Stones were also used, or they were used first, after which the fighters moved in closer against their rivals with their sticks. Faction fighting was a feature of fairs around the country, as well as of many other gatherings of the public during the nineteenth century. The fights might be due to insults or grievances, real or perceived, and tended to involve the same families, neighbours, political allies or sectarian groups, who fought against each other regularly.

A serious fight took place on the fair day of 11 August 1813, as summarised by the *Freeman's Journal*:

> A serious riot took place at the fair of Killorglin, on Wednesday last, the particulars of which have not yet come to our knowledge; we understand that the military were implicated,[133] and that several shots were fired; one man named Connor was shot dead, and several others dangerously wounded, both from the firing and the showers of stones which flew in every direction.[134]

Historian of Killorglin Kieran Foley quoted a police report of a faction fight which took place on the second day of the fair of 1837:

> This day about half past five in the afternoon, two factions, the Foleys – and Dodds and Kearins, and their several adherents came in contact and commenced fighting with sticks in the lower part of the village near the bridge. Sub-Constable Haugh and I, with some others of the peacable inhabitants had got them separated when they burst from the houses and lanes, and commenced throwing stones in a most furious and savage manner. The Foley faction being the more numerous they beat the other faction up the street, for about half an hour at least. There were four persons nearly killed on the spot who are in a dangerous state … There have been several windows and doors broken with stones … Several persons are in dread to stop in their houses this night and some have left the village. I have succeeded in taking down several names of the most active, but was obliged to run off several times.[135]

Kieran Foley added, 'One man, Thomas Daly, died as a result of that fight. Using tongs as a weapon, he had been very much involved in the fighting. But one of his opponents took the tongs from him and then hit him with it. He died a few weeks later from his injuries.'[136]

Some of the faction fights in Killorglin were run on party-political lines. Michael 'Big Mick' Foley and his allies were supporters of the Conservative party, and in 1837 they campaigned vigorously for Arthur Blennerhassett among the small number of county freeholders who were entitled to vote.[137] The county election of 1837 was held in early August, in an atmosphere of some animosity, because the opposing party were the Whigs. These were allied to the celebrated Daniel O'Connell (1775-1847) and his movement for the repeal of the Act of Union between the parliaments of Britain and Ireland. O'Connell had previously achieved Catholic Emancipation, the removal of various prohibitions imposed upon Irish Catholics. This set the Foley faction at odds with the local Catholic clergy and the supporters of O'Connell. Michael's brother had chaired a public meeting in Killorglin in January opposing the use of the church building for electioneering purposes by their opponents.[138] His nephew, Michael O'Sullivan, had been attacked by supporters of Fr O'Connor on 6 August, when he strode in front of the priest as he was giving an election speech at a table in the street, sticking his hands in his pockets and calling for 'a boo for the priest'.[139] The party confrontations continued on 12 August:

> ... as some freeholders in the interest of Mr Blennerhassett were return-ing from Tralee, passing through the village of Killorglin, some stones were thrown at them; this act of violence brought up some friends of Mr Michael James Foley, to their aid and protection, when they were attacked by the hostile faction, and a riot ensued, which ended in the defeat of the assailing party.[140]

Michael Foley himself may not have been involved in these particular episodes; by 1835 he was described in a police report as 'formerly a notorious rioter and leader of a faction'.[141] His fighting days may have been during the election campaigns of 1818 and afterwards; at his death in January 1867 an obituary noted that: 'He was always prepared some 50 years ago ... to maintain the pre-eminence of his party, either single-handed or at the head of his friends ... he took an earnest and most active part in the desperate election contests that were held in this county ... as an ally to the landlord and Conservative party'.[142]

The Foley faction were nicknamed 'the Foulue party'[143] or 'the Foulowos',[144] following the Irish pronunciation of the surname, O'Foghlú. Their opponents were identified by the *Cork Examiner* in 1846 as 'the Pallatines', but the reason behind this name is less easy to interpret; the Palatines had been Protestants from various European countries who had been encouraged to settle on Irish estates by landlords anxious to increase the population of Protestant tenants, and some of them settled in Kerry.

It is possible that the goat of the fair was a mascot for the Foley faction fighters, as puck goats were traditionally associated with bucking, butting and kicking. The mascot may also have been displayed on several other occasions during the year at gatherings of the faction, which became fore-shortened to one occasion, the fair only; a report by the *Cork Examiner* appears to suggest that the custom of displaying the goat had been neglected so that it had come to be displayed only when it was decorated as the king of the fair: 'The ancient custom, which was at one time sacrilege, or cowardice to neglect, has now so far degenerated, that the outlawed animal is only beautified in his temporary regalities'.[145] The fact that the goat was described as 'outlawed' also seems to suggest that it was identified with illegal activities. In the same way that army regiments often parade a dog as a mascot, perhaps the Foley faction displayed a puck goat as theirs.

Faction fights were condemned by the clergy and opposed by the police, and gradually the practice died out. Nevertheless, stick fighting at the fair continued to occur sporadically. A fight took place at the fair of 1846, although the factions were not identified; 'It was so desperately ferocious that the police force available did not think it prudent, as I am informed, to interfere'.[146] In 1893, 'A serious row took place at "Puck" fair on Friday between a number of young men from Currans and Glenbeigh. Sticks were freely used and a force of police with drawn batons had to be requisitioned to quiet the row. A number of men had their heads cut'.[147]

THE GOAT DISPLAY

The buying, selling, sightseeing, eating, drinking and fighting of the fair all took place under the patronage of the puck goat. He was always referred to as if he was a royal character; 'the King of the Fair', 'the Mountain Prince', 'The Lord of the Fair', or 'King Puck'.[148]

At first the goat seems to have been simply paraded around the fair, as stated by the *Topographical Dictionary of Ireland* in 1837.[149] In 1841, it was first displayed from an elevated position: 'On former occasions … the horned monarch was permitted to stand on mother earth. Not so on the present', wrote the *Kerry Evening Post* in that year, and according to what were described as 'the improved tastes' of those 'who presided over the festive

A close-up of the Puck Fair goat, 1983. (© Martin Parr. Courtesy of Magnum Photos)

exhibition', the goat was installed in 'a crate well secured upon a lofty poll,[150] where the animal might be seen … bowing to the admiring crowds with all the dignity of a newly-elected MP'.[151] (The latter comment was a gibe at the election activities of the Foley faction.)

A report in the *Cork Examiner* from 1846 suggests that the ceremonies were performed after Michael Foley was paid a fee. The animal was displayed at the fair 'when "Big Mick", to whom the hereditary revenue of the fair belongs, has got a caubeen[152] full of half crowns for custom', after which the peasantry led forth the goat.[153] Occasionally, no goat was displayed. Even in 1837, the *Topographical Dictionary of Ireland* said that the goat was only sometimes paraded around the fair; and no goat was shown at the fair of 1847. No explanation was reported for this absence in press reports: the 1847 fair may have lacked the goat element as some consequence of the Great Famine (1845-1849); specifically, it may have been considered to be an inappropriate frivolity given the suffering of the country.

Later, the goat was generally displayed from the battlements of the Blennerhassett family mansion, formerly Castle Conway. Samuel Hussey said that the goat was attached to the flagpole of the castle.[154] The Mullins family did not reside at the castle they had bought from the Blennerhassetts, and instead rented it out; the last tenant was Fr Louney, who died in 1844.[155] It may have been after his death, when the building was empty, that the goat began to be raised upon the castle itself; this may be significant, because Fr Louney had been an opponent of the Foley faction – at the public meeting held in January 1837 there had been cries of 'boo for Louney! Down with tyranny!'[156] and placing their emblem (if it was such) upon his former residence might have represented their literally lording it over him posthumously. Unusually, two goats were shown in 1863: one on the castle, and one on a stand in the centre of the town. The following year a goat was placed on one battlement of the castle and a statue of a mounted horseman was placed on another.[157]

In 1869 the building was badly damaged after a failed attempt to demolish it and replace it with a courthouse.[158] Accordingly, in 1870, the 4th Baron Ventry, Dayrolles Blakeney Mullins (1828-1914), established a wooden stage for the animal in the centre of the town; the appearance of this structure was apparently intended to recall to mind the impression of the former castle-tower display.[159] The platform was formed by four long poles, strapped together in a square shape, with a stage created in the middle with some rough planks. A photograph of the stand taken for the Lawrence photographic studio of Dublin, sometime between 1880 and 1900, shows it as having two tiers, with the goat placed on the top tier.[160] The structure was almost always described as 20-25ft tall, but a taller stage, of about 40ft, seems to have been constructed from about 1908.[161] The stands were decorated with branches of evergreen foliage.

In 1873, the platform was erected at the entrance to the fair field; to judge from maps of the town from 1854 and 1894, the entrance appears to have been situated at the corner of the field where Mill Road and Upper Bridge Street meet.[162] For a brief time the stand may have been placed directly opposite this entrance, at a spot where a ball alley later stood, and which is now Library Place.[163] In 1877 the stand was placed beside the old castle.[164] In following years, it was returned to the town square, where it has remained ever since.

It is not clear if the goat for display was caught wild. The King of the Fair, 'from time immemorial, has been the largest Buck Goat which the mountains of Iveragh can produce', wrote the *Kerry Evening Post* in 1841. Other reports seem to suggest that the goats were chosen from among domesticated animals; and sometimes the same goat may have been used more than once:

a report of 1865 appeared to hint that the dethroned goat was kept over to be presented again the following year.[165]

Accounts describe the animal as being decorated with green and red ribbons, and with flowers.[166] Adding the ribbons seems to have been done by young women; the goat was 'ornamented with gaudy ribbons – the gift of many a rustic fair one to the Mountain Prince'.[167] Press reports give the impression that a white goat seems to have been preferred for display, but this was never stated outright.[168]

The goat spent the duration of the fair in a cage, described as made of iron or wood,[169] with a canopy to protect him from the elements and a supply of cabbages and water to sustain him. The cage is first mentioned in 1877, but it may have dated to earlier decades. The goat was secured by a collar, or chained by each horn,[170] and he sometimes had a bell, or two bells, attached to his horns.[171]

The enthronement was almost always done on the afternoon of the 10th (although in 1909 it was performed on the evening of the 9th). The animal was hoisted up to the top of the stand by men using ropes and pulleys attached to the cage. At the fair of 1913, 'The poles had not arrived in time to have the pulleys affixed,' explained the Killorglin correspondent of the *Kerryman*, 'and so the best had to be made of things as they were on the occasion, though it was perhaps a little rough on the Hero'.[172] How rough, exactly, was described in a letter to the *Irish Independent*:

The goat was placed in a cage-like structure and appeared to be roped to the sides of it. Four 'men' on the first landing of the platform held a rope affixed to a lath in the cage, and, with a little assistance from a few boys on the ground attempted to hoist the unfortunate 'puck'. The affair was accompanied by the inspiring strains of a brass band and the cheering of an enormous crowd. But any thoughtful person can imagine what the poor animal suffered when I state it took 35 minutes to transport him from terra firma to an altitude of about 40 feet. The mechanism of the pully was ignored, and the bottom falling out of the cage the struggles and cries of the 'puck' were pitiable in the extreme. Several visitors and townspeople, in my presence, expressed their disgust at the torture inflicted on the 'hero of the fair' on witnessing his unfortunate plight.[173]

The goat stage was sometimes illuminated all night with oil lamps. In 1870 the platform was adorned with coloured lanterns, which cast their light into the distance of the countryside, creating a romantic impression.[174] In 1912 the stand was hung with a number of red storm lanterns.[175] Electricity was first generated for Killorglin in 1916, and for at least part of the nights of that year's fair, electric lights decorated the goat platform.[176]

Banners were attached to the goat stage, or stretched across the main streets; first mentioned in the 1860s.[177] Many of these were simple welcome messages, but there were other kinds too. Visitors to the fair of 1870 would have smiled to see a banner with the words, 'Let Go My Leg', a phrase drawn from the popular song 'The Peeler and the Goat':

Meg a meg let go of me leg
Or I'll pucker you with me horn oh!
Fiddle dee dee let go of me
Or I'll leave you bruised and torn oh!

The song had originally been written around 1830 by Darby Ryan, of Bansha, County Tipperary, to ridicule the first policemen who were introduced to Ireland by Sir Robert Peel, Chief Secretary for Ireland, the policemen thereafter becoming known as Peelers. In the song a policeman tries to arrest a goat for loitering. It became hugely popular and numerous variations of the original lyrics were devised. It continued to be associated with Puck Fair, and was recited by a young girl at the goat enthronement of 1956.[178]

In 1908, when the young men of the Total Abstinence Society began to take over the running of the goat celebration, they added their own banner, '*Eire gan Meisge, Eire gan Spleadeacas*' (Ireland Sober is Ireland Free).

Flags were also attached to the goat stand. In 1873, there was a single flag 'of red, white and blue',[179] which can be interpreted to have been a representation of the colours of the British Empire. Flags flown in 1908 included the green flag of Ireland, the Stars and Stripes of the United States, and a flag of 'Blue, White and Red', afterwards described as the French flag.[180] From 1910, the Irish-American fraternal organisation the Ancient Order of Hibernians sent over an American flag for display, until the practice was discontinued in the 1930s.[181]

THE DETHRONEMENT CEREMONY

At all times, a parade and a ceremony accompanied the goat dethronement, as it had the enthronement. Anthony Walsh, writing of the origins and customs of the fair in 1955, quoted a letter from a Mrs O.F. Doyle, to the *Kerry Sentinel*, which he did not date (although that newspaper ceased publication in 1918): 'He is saddled and taken round the town on the shoulders of four strapping lads, and after collecting his dues from the ever willing shopkeepers, is sold by auction, the local bellman claiming the fees'.[182]

For the fair of 1908, a new song, 'Long Live King Puck', was composed by a local musician, and played as the goat was lowered from the platform. The following year the dethronement became a truly grand event in itself; the temperance society brass band played from their rooms in Lower Bridge Street to the square;

> … and the King, whose time had now come, was lowered from his dignified position and, still in the throne, was conveyed through the streets in a most becoming wagonette drawn by a handsome pair of horses of a steel grey colour and driven by a coachman in green livery. This was a most uncommon sight in itself, but then the band played after the royal wagonette and the crowd followed through the streets until they took him to the Rooms, and Puck Fair was over – passed for another year.[183]

Notes

1 Samuel Lewis, *A Topographical Dictionary of Ireland* Vol. II (S. Lewis & Co., London, 1837) page 152.
2 G.J. Lyne, 'Rev Daniel A. Beaufort's Tour of Kerry, 1778', *Kerry Archaeological and Historical Society Journal*, xviii (1985). Quoted in Kieran Foley, *History of Killorglin* (1988) page 122.
3 Thomas Reid, *Travels in Ireland in the year 1822* (Longman, London, 1823). Quoted in Kieran Foley, *History of Killorglin* (1988) page 122.
4 'Puck Fair', *Tralee Chronicle*, 12 August 1870.
5 'Puck Fair', *Tralee Chronicle*, 14 August 1863.
6 'Puck Fair', *Tralee Chronicle*, 15 August 1865. This report mentions the Ventry Arms.
7 *Freeman's Journal*, 16 September 1874.
8 'Killorglin (Puck) Fair', *Kerry Sentinel*, 21 August 1912; 'Puck Fair', *Kerryman*, 23 August 1913.
9 'Irish Fairs to be Held During the Ensuing Week', *Freeman's Journal*, 8 August 1840.
10 'Puck Fair', *Kerry Sentinel*, 13 August 1898.

11 'Puck Fair', *Kerry Sentinel*, 17 August 1901.

12 'Puck Fair', *Tralee Chronicle*, 14 August 1857.

13 Robert Lynd, *Rambles in Ireland* (Mills and Boon, London, 1912) pages 161-162.

14 'Puck Fair', *Tralee Chronicle*, 14 August 1857; 'Puck Fair – Yesterday', *Tralee Chronicle*, 13 August 1861.

15 'Big Hosting at Puck Fair', *Nenagh Guardian*, 15 August 1953. The article noted that the goat was provided by Michael Houlihan 'for the 52nd year' (i.e since 1901); 'Thought of My Coronation Makes Me Feel Just Like a Kid Again', *Kerryman*, 6 August 1960. Michael Houlihan was the contractor to the Puck Fair committee 'for 56 years' (i.e since 1904).

16 'Puck Fair', *Tralee Chronicle*, 12 August 1873.

17 Samuel Lewis, *A Topographical Dictionary of Ireland* Vol. II (S. Lewis & Co., London, 1837) page 152.

18 Near Tralee.

19 Near Farranfore.

20 'Murderous Assault', *Irish Times*, 16 August 1862.

21 'Scandalous Outrage', *Irish Times*, 23 August 1862.

22 'Ireland', *Essex Standard*, 20 August 1862.

23 1841 Census. Quoted in Kieran Foley, *History of Killorglin* (1988) page 33.

24 Kieran Foley, *History of Killorglin* (1988) page 126.

25 'Puck Fair', *Tralee Chronicle*, 12 August 1862.

26 'Puck Fair', *Tralee Chronicle*, 12 August 1873.

27 'Puck Fair', *Kerry Sentinel*, 18 August 1888.

28 Lady Gordon, *The Winds of Time* (John Murray, London, 1934) pages 126-127.

29 'Puck Fair', *Tralee Chronicle*, 14 August 1863.

30 'Killorglin Great Annual Fair', *Kerry Sentinel*, 14 August 1883.

31 J.M. Synge, *In Wicklow, West Kerry and Connemara* (Maunsell, Dublin, 1911) page 121.

32 Ann Saddlemyer (ed.), *The Collected Letters of John Millington Synge, Vol 1 1871-1907* (Clarendon Press, Oxford, 1983) page 92.

33 J.M. Synge, *In Wicklow, West Kerry and Connemara* (Maunsell, Dublin, 1911) page 122.

34 'Serious Accident at "Puck" Fair', *Kerry Sentinel*, 13 August 1904.

35 'Killorglin (Puck) Fair', *Kerry Sentinel*, 19 August 1911.

36 'Puck Fair', *Tralee Chronicle*, 14 August 1863.

37 'Puck Fair', *Kerry Sentinel*, 17 August 1901.

38 Windham Thomas Wyndham-Quin (1841-1926), 4th Earl of Dunraven and Mount-Earl. The family had an estate at Adare Manor, County Limerick.

39 'Puck Fair', *Tralee Chronicle*, 12 August 1873.

40 *Freeman's Journal*, 18 August 1825.

41 Twenty.

42 A rope that fitted around the horse's head, enabling it to be led around.

43 Samuel Lewis, *A Topographical Dictionary of Ireland*,Vol. II (S. Lewis and Co., London, 1837) page 44.

44 *Ibid*.

45 'Puck Fair', *Tralee Chronicle*, 12 August 1873.

46 'Puck' Fair', *Kerry Sentinel*, 16 August 1878.

47 'Puck Fair', *Tralee Chronicle*, 17 August 1850.

48 *Tralee Chronicle*, 15 August 1856.

49 A commonly used description, also attributed to Indian nationalist leader Mahatma Gandhi.

50 'Killorglin Great Fair', *Kerry Examiner*, 12 August 1845.

51 '"Puck" Fair', *Kerry Sentinel*, 16 August 1913.

52 Patrick Houlihan, *Cast a Laune Shadow: Reminiscences of Life in Killorglin* (1997) page 119.

53 'Large Pig Fair in Killorglin', *Kerry Sentinel*, 14 August 1895.

54 'Puck Fair', *Kerry Sentinel*, 13 August 1898.

55 'Puck Fair', *Kerry Sentinel*, 13 August 1898.

56 Donnacha Seán Lucey, *Land, Popular Politics and Agrarian Violence in Ireland: The Case of County Kerry, 1872-86* (University College Dublin Press, Dublin, 2011) page 12.

57 Lady Gordon, *The Mists of Time* (John Murray, London, 1934) page 129.

58 'Puck Fair', *Tralee Chronicle*, 14 August 1877.

59 'The Irishman. A Novel Purchase', *Penny Illustrated Paper and Illustrated Times*, 25 August 1883.

60 'Puck Fair', *Tralee Chronicle*, 14 August 1857.

61 'Puck Fair', *Tralee Chronicle*, 13 August 1875; 'The Land Agitation. Meeting in Killorglin', *Kerry Sentinel*, 13 August 1880.

62 J.M. Synge, *In Wicklow, West Kerry and Connemara* (Maunsell, Dublin, 1911) page 122.

63 'Pars from Puck', *Kerryman*, 21 August 1909.

64 'Puck Fair', *Tralee Chronicle*, 12 August 1873.

65 'Killorglin (Puck) Fair', *Kerry Sentinel*, 21 August 1912.

66 'Pars from Puck', *Kerryman*, 22 August 1908.

67 'Killorglin Great Fair', *Kerry Examiner*, 12 August 1845.

68 'Puck Fair – Yesterday', *Tralee Chronicle*, 13 August 1861.

69 *Ibid.*

70 'Pars from Puck', *Kerryman*, 15 August 1908; 'Bantry August Fair', *Southern Star*, 26 August 1905.

71 M.C.J., 'Puck Fair', *Tralee Chronicle*, 17 August 1850.

72 Sweepstakes: the total sum of money wagered by all. 'Quart' may refer to a unit of alcohol, either beer or whiskey.

73 Worn-out old horses.

74 Vanguard: the frontrunners.

75 M.C.J., '"Puck" Fair', *Tralee Chronicle*, 14 August 1847.

76 M.C.J., '"Puck" Fair', *Tralee Chronicle*, 17 August 1850.

77 'Puck Fair – Yesterday', *Tralee Chronicle*, 13 August 1861; 'Puck Fair', *Tralee Chronicle*, 14 August 1863; 'Puck Fair – Yesterday', *Tralee Chronicle*, 12 August 1864.

78 The writer introduced a distinction in brackets to distinguish the Traveller family of Foleys from the Foleys of Anglont, Barons of Puck Fair.

79 Kenmare Fair, always held on 15 August.

80 'Pars from Puck', *Kerryman*, 15 August 1908.

81 Over a week afterwards.

82 Milltown Sports day was held on 15 August.

83 'Pars from Puck', *Kerryman*, 21 August 1909.

84 Policemen.

85 Walter Starkie, *Scholars and Gypsies* (John Murray, London, 1963) page 25.

86 'Round the World and Home', *Irish Times*, 11 July 1931. The event described was not dated to any particular year, but we suspect it to date to before the turn of the century.

87 The term 'foreigners' was used to denote people from other counties. *See* 'The Land Agitation. Meeting in Killorglin', *Kerry Sentinel*, 13 August 1880: 'Puck Fair' brings together literally the whole 'Kingdom of Kerry', with a goodly sprinkling of 'foreigners' from the neighbouring counties of Cork, Limerick, and Clare'.

88 'Puck Fair', *Kerry Sentinel*, 16 August 1913.

89 'Puck Fair', *Tralee Chronicle*, 13 August 1875.

90 *A new Song called the Star of Slane, to which are added, the Downfall of Trade, and the Tinware Lass* (Drogheda, 1826).

91 The Russo-Japanese War ran from February 1904 until September 1905. It was a struggle between two imperial powers for access and influence in the Pacific region. Japan emerged victorious.

92 The Crimean War (1853-1856) was fought between Russia and the British Empire (and her allies). Much of the fighting took place on the Crimean Peninsula, on the northern side of the Black Sea. Many Irish soldiers took part and 7000 were killed.

93 J.M. Synge, *In Wicklow, West Kerry and Connemara* (Maunsell, Dublin, 1911) page 126.

94 'Puck Fair', *Kerry Sentinel*, 17 August 1901.

95 'Puck Fair', *Tralee Chronicle*, 17 August 1850.

96 J.M. Synge, *In Wicklow, West Kerry and Connemara* (Maunsell, Dublin, 1911) page 121.

97 J.M. Synge, *In Wicklow, West Kerry and Connemara. Essays by George Gmelch and Ann Saddlemyer* (O'Brien Press, Dublin, 1980) pages 25-26.

98 Robert Lynd, *Rambles in Ireland* (Mills and Boon, London, 1912) page 151.

99 'Puck Fair', *Tralee Chronicle*, 13 August 1875.

100 William Makepeace Thackeray, *The Irish Sketch Book* (Smith, Elder and Co., London, 1869) page 121.

101 'Puck Fair', *Tralee Chronicle*, 12 August 1862; 'Puck Fair', *Tralee Chronicle*, 12 August 1873.

102 Robert Lynd, *Rambles in Ireland* (Mills and Boon, London, 1912) pages 154-156.

103 *Charitable and Public Institutions; Tolls and Customs. Accounts and Papers relating to Ireland Vol 8* (1830) pages 91-92. Killorglin's fair is not listed in the survey.

104 Robert Lynd, *Rambles in Ireland* (Mills and Boon, London, 1912) pages 157-158.

105 *Ibid.* page 160.

106 Lady Gordon, *The Winds of Time* (John Murray, London, 1934) page 127.

107 'Puck Fair', *Tralee Chronicle*, 12 August 1862.

108 J.M. Synge, *In Wicklow, West Kerry and Connemara* (Maunsell, Dublin, 1911) page 124.

109 'Puck Fair', *Tralee Chronicle*, 12 August 1873.

110 Robert Lynd, *Rambles in Ireland* (Mills and Boon, London, 1912) page 163.

111 The article from which the description is taken also refers to an old woman 'with the fortune-telling birds'. In this diversion a stallholder typically presented a small rack of folded papers, which two pet birds were invited to peck at; the folded papers they picked contained a written or printed message for the customer. At the Listowel Fair writer Bryan MacMahon (1909-1998) as a child saw 'budgerigars picking out fortunes for giggling country girls'. (Bryan MacMahon, 'Born in a Market Place', in *Kerry Through Its Writers*, ed. Gabriel Fitzmaurice (New Island, Dublin, 1993) page 94.)

112 'Killorglin Puck', *Kerryman*, 5 September 1908.

113 'Puck Fair', *Tralee Chronicle*, 14 August 1877.

114 M.C.K., 'Puck Fair', *The Irish Monthly*, Vol. 22, July 1894, page 374.

115 Michael Houlihan, *Puck Fair History and Traditions* (Treaty Press, Limerick, 1999) page 105.

116 'Charge of Shooting at Killorglin', *Kerryman*, 26 August 1905.

117 J.M. Synge, *In Wicklow, West Kerry and Connemara* (Maunsell, Dublin, 1911) page 121.

118 'Puck Fair – Yesterday', *Tralee Chronicle*, 12 August 1864; 'Puck Fair', *Tralee Chronicle*, 12 August 1862.

119 'Puck Fair', *Tralee Chronicle*, 17 August 1850.

120 Robert Lynd, *Rambles in Ireland* (Mills and Boon, London, 1912) page 150.

121 Lady Gordon, *The Winds of Time* (John Murray, London, 1934) page 125.

122 'Puck Fair – Yesterday', *Tralee Chronicle*, 12 August 1864.

123 J.G. O'Keeffe, 'A Great Horse Fair', *The Land Magazine*, January 1899, pages 85-86.

124 'Puck Fair', *Tralee Chronicle*, 17 August 1850.

125 'Puck Fair', *Kerry Sentinel*, 16 August 1878.

126 'Fearful Scene on a Railway Platform in Kerry', *Kildare Observer*, 17 August 1895.

127 Liam Foley, 'Puck – The Mardi Gras of the South', *Kerryman*, 11 August 1945. Note: we place this story in the late 1800s based on the absence of Michael Doolan from the Census of 1901 and the Census of 1911; and Mr Foley's noting, in 1945, that the incident 'happened many years ago within the memory of only the oldest of our inhabitants'.

128 S.M. Hussey, *Reminiscences of an Irish Land Agent* (Duckworth, London, 1904) page 105.

129 'Puck Fair', *Kerry Sentinel*, 17 August 1901.

130 'Pars from Puck', *Kerryman*, 22 August 1908.

131 'Pars from Puch', *Kerryman*, 21 August 1909.

132 Patrick Logan, *Fair Day: The Story of Irish Fairs and Markets* (Appletree Press, Belfast, 1986) page 103.

133 Implicated: involved. The word did not then carry connotations of culpability. Kieran Foley noted that troops from Milltown fired 120 rounds of ammunition during the riot. (Kieran Foley, *History of Killorglin* (1988) page 39.)

134 *Freeman's Journal*, 19 August 1813.

135 Police report of Constable Isaac Bingham, 12 August 1837. Quoted in Kieran Foley, *History of Killorglin* (1988) page 41.

136 Kieran Foley, *History of Killorglin* (1988) page 41.

137 'Ireland. Death of Mr Michael James Foley, of Killorglin', *Dorset Chronicle*, 31 January 1867. (Reprinted from the *Kerry Evening Post*.)

138 'Meeting at Killorglan, County Kerry', *London Standard*, 10 February 1837. (Report abridged from the *Kerry Evening Post*.)

139 'Killorglan Petty Sessions', *Freeman's Journal*, 2 September 1837.

140 *Kerry Evening Post*, 16 August 1837.

141 Kieran Foley, *History of Killorglin* (1988) page 41.

142 Ireland. Death of Mr Michael James Foley, of Killorglin', *Dorset Chronicle*, 31 January 1867. (Reprinted from the *Kerry Evening Post*.)

143 'Killorglan Petty Sessions', *Freeman's Journal*, 2 September 1837.

144 'Puck Fair', *Cork Examiner*, 17 August 1846.

145 *Ibid.*

146 *Ibid.*

147 'Row at "Puck' Fair"', *Kerry Sentinel*, 16 August 1893.

148 'Puck Fair', *Kerry Evening Post*, 11 August 1841; '"Puck" Fair', *Tralee Chronicle*, August 14, 1847; '"Puck" Fair', *Tralee Chronicle*, 16 August 1851; '"Puck' Fair', *Kerry Sentinel*, August 16, 1878.

149 Samuel Lewis, *A Topographical Dictionary of Ireland* Vol. II (S. Lewis and Co., London, 1837) page 152.

150 Poll: pole.

151 'Puck Fair', *Kerry Evening Post*, 11 August 1841.

152 *cáibín*: cap or beret.

153 'Puck Fair', *Cork Examiner*, 17 August 1846.

154 S.M. Hussey, *Reminiscences of an Irish Land Agent* (Duckworth, London, 1904) page 104.

155 Valerie Bary, *Houses of Kerry* (Ballinakella Press, County Clare, 1994) page 154.

156 'Meeting at Killorglan, County Kerry', *London Standard*, 10 February 1837. (Report abridged from the *Kerry Evening Post*.)

157 'Puck Fair – Yesterday', *Tralee Chronicle*, 12 August 1864.

158 Michael Houlihan, *Puck Fair History and Traditions* (Treaty Press, Limerick, 1999) page 26.

159 M.C.K., 'Puck Fair', *The Irish Monthly*, Vol. 22, July 1894, page 375

160 These can be viewed at the National Library of Ireland website, www.nli.ie.

161 'Pars from Puck', *Kerryman*, 15 August 1908; 'Pars from Puck', *Kerryman*, 21 August 1909.

162 Kieran Foley, *History of Killorglin* (1988) page 126.

163 'Oldest and Most Colourful Fair in the Country', *Kerryman*, 6 August 1955.

164 'Puck Fair', *Tralee Chronicle*, 14 August 1877.

165 'Puck Fair', *Tralee Chronicle*, 15 August 1865. 'He had equal honors last year and very good depasturing since in the capital hotel 'the Ventry Arms' Killorglin, where no doubt he will receive equal fare until called upon next year'.

166 'Puck Fair', *Tralee Chronicle*, 16 August 1851; 'Puck Fair', *Tralee Chronicle*, 14 August 1857.

167 'Puck Fair', *Tralee Chronicle*, 14 August 1847. The reporter was recalling how the goat was presented; there was no goat displayed in 1847.

168 'Puck Fair', *Tralee Chronicle*, 16 August 1851; 'Puck Fair – Yesterday', *Tralee Chronicle*, 13 August 1861.

169 'Puck Fair', *Tralee Chronicle*, 14 August 1877; M.C.K., 'Puck Fair', *The Irish Monthly*, Vol. 22, July 1894, page 374.

170 M.C.K., 'Puck Fair', *The Irish Monthly*, Vol. 22, July 1894, page 374; J.M. Synge, *In Wicklow, West Kerry and Connemara* (Maunsell, Dublin, 1911) page 122

171 'Puck Fair', *Tralee Chronicle*, 14 August 1863; 'Puck Fair', *Kerry Sentinel*, 16 August 1913.

172 'Puck Fair', *Kerryman*, 23 August 1913.

173 'Puck Fair at Killorglin'. Letter from Eamon O'Ceiris, Scartaglen, Co Kerry. *Irish Independent*, 16 August 1913.

174 'Puck Fair', *Tralee Chronicle*, 12 August 1870.

175 Robert Lynd, *Rambles in Ireland* (Mills and Boon, London, 1912) page 146.

176 'A Midnight Scene at Puck', *Kerryman*, 26 August 1916.

177 'Puck Fair – Yesterday', *Tralee Chronicle*, 12 August 1864.

178 'Bad Weather Made Little Difference to Puck Fair', *Kerryman*, 18 August 1956.

179 'Puck Fair', *Tralee Chronicle*, 12 August 1873.

180 'Pars from Puck', *Kerryman*, 15 August 1908; 'Killorglin Puck', *Kerryman*, 5 September 1908.

181 Patrick Houlihan, *Cast a Laune Shadow: Reminiscences of Life in Killorglin* (1997) page 152.

182 Anthony Walsh, 'The Origin of Puck Fair', in *The Irishman's Annual* (Michael Glazier, Tralee, 1955) page 59.

183 'Pars from Puck', *Kerryman*, 21 August 1909.

3

Puck Fair and the National Questions

Between 1800 and 1922, the various Irish social, economic and national issues of the period naturally impacted upon the fair. Moreover, the event sometimes became an arena in which some of these issues were played out in public.

Puck Fair and the Tithe War

Tillage farmers not only had to pay rent to landlords or their middlemen, they were also subject to various fees due to the Catholic clergy on the one hand, and to tithes, a proportion of the value of their crops that had to be paid to the Church of Ireland, on the other. Those farmers who grazed cattle were exempt from tithes.

To oppose these payments, a secret agrarian organisation, The Rightboys, formed in County Cork in 1785. The movement quickly spread to County Kerry and became active in 1786. Sometimes it bound people by oaths not to pay dues and tithes, and employed physical intimidation to enforce its commands, travelling at night to the homes of those suspected of paying. Alternatively, it set the maximum rates that were to be paid to Catholic priests for the ceremonies of marriage, baptism, visiting the sick and hearing confession.

On Thursday, 10 August 1786, a party of Rightboys, 'with pipers playing and horns sounding', erected a gallows 'with a rope suspended from the

centre, near the bridge of Killorglin, where the fair was on the following day
held, on which were placed labels, expressive of the fate which was sure to
await any person who dared to transgress their rules'.[1] Remarkably, it was
left to stand until at least the following Monday.

The Rightboy movement in the county faded by 1787, but opposition
sprang up again in Killorglin between 1816 and 1822. Michael 'Big Mick'
Foley, the Baron of the Fair, was awakened on a November night in 1820 by
a number of men, and, according to a magistrates' report:

> ... forcibly compelled to take an oath, to pay no more money to a priest
> at any wedding he should be at than one shilling ... not to give the horses
> of priests oats, and to give priests at stations[2] their breakfasts only and no
> whiskey or any other kinds of spirits, and also to particularly adhere to
> every other regulation of the parishioners to curtail in a fair and regular
> manner the dues of priests.[3]

Tithes payable to the Church of Ireland were also objected to during
the 1820s, but a determined national campaign against them did not
begin until the 1830s. They were vigorously opposed by the priests and
the people of Killorglin, as elsewhere, and the Tithe War (1831-1836),
the campaign of non-payment, was later stated to be one of the origins of
the goat ceremony of Puck Fair: a goat seized by bailiffs collecting farm
animals in lieu of payment broke away and returned to the town, and was
feted ever since.

PUCK FAIR AND THE FAMINE

Contradictory contemporary reports make it difficult to assess the impact
of the years of the Great Famine (1845-1849) and its aftermath upon the
people of Killorglin and on Puck Fair.

In 1846 a representative of the Mullins family estates wrote of the ravaged
potato crops, so that 'The fields in Kerry look as if fire had passed over
them'.[4] In January 1847, the *Kerry Examiner* reported that: 'The people of
Killorglin are in a state of the direst destitution'.

Half the labouring population cannot procure employment; and those employed find it impossible to support their families, the amount of their wages being miserably disproportionate to the price of food. They are therefore becoming completely exhausted. Our informant, a clergyman from the district, vividly described for us the sufferings of the poor ... Particular instances of suffering and death which he described were truly shocking. In one miserable cabin which he visited a few days ago, there were four, the father and mother and a full grown young man and woman huddled together – the mother dead and the others in the agony of death! ... Numbers, this gentleman informed us, may be seen crawling with swollen limbs and bodies, in the very last stage of existence.[5]

Yet visiting inspectors regularly claimed there were frequent irregularities in the administration of relief in the parish, and that people were being fed who had no need of assistance. In 1848, one of the Killorglin officials even cited the case of a mule, which had been fed meal intended for the relief of the destitute.[6]

Puck Fair carried on during the years of the Famine, with little at first to suggest extreme hardship. In 1847, generally considered to be a peak year of distress nationally, the Killorglin correspondent of the *Tralee Chronicle* said, 'Although usually much crowded, I never saw it so thronged', while 'An immense quantity of stock of every description was presented for sale'.[7] In 1848, 'The attendance of persons in search of fun was most numerous, notwithstanding the wetness of the day'.[8]

By 1849, however, things had changed: the fair was 'one of the worst that had been remembered'; 'Better was anticipated, but the prices of every species of stock were discouragingly low, and the people's spirits sunk and dejected'.[9] The fair of 1850 was also 'one of the worst for the farmer remembered for many years', and while there was plenty of stock on offer, 'demand was slack and prices were low'.[10] At the same time, potato crops everywhere were ruined by blight; in nearby Milltown, 'The potato crop is gone. In every garden here at least half of them are diseased',[11] while in Dingle, 'The potatoes are worse here this year than they ever were'.[12]

The year 1851 seems to have marked the beginning of a recovery. 'We have been through a considerable portion of the south of the County during the last ten days,' wrote the editor of the *Tralee Chronicle*, before going on to say:

… and in every quarter, we were grieved to perceive, the potato fields were black … In no place, notwithstanding, have we seen a diseased potato. On the contrary we have seen some very fine ones being dug, and the answers to our queries in all quarters were that the tubers were very good. On the whole, our accounts from other parts of the County are in accordance with our own observation, and we are still led to hope that, though much will be lost, yet that there will be a comparatively fair crop.[13]

At the same time, Puck Fair, 'though falling far short of the fairs of olden times, was, considering that we have "fallen upon evil days" not a bad one'.[14]

The factor of social class was important in determining both who suffered most and for how long Puck Fair continued largely unaffected. The tenant farmers had animals to sell at the fair, which brought in cash that could be used to buy food, even if prices rose. In contrast, many working labourers were often paid by farmers by being given a potato patch: when the crops failed, they had no access to money to buy food. Then there was the reserve army of under-employed labourers who had neither a garden nor money: they had to resort to the workhouse, where they might die of disease, or they could tramp the roads in search of scarce opportunities for work. Historian of Killorglin Kieran Foley concluded, 'The population of the town itself fell quite dramatically. It went from 925 in 1841 down to 590 in 1851, and in that same ten-year period the number of inhabited houses in the town dropped from 160 to 109'.[15] That drop in urban population was almost certainly to do with labourers and their families, who comprised most of the town dwellers.

PUCK FAIR AND THE LAND QUESTION

For many Irish political campaigners, the worst effects of the Great Famine were considered to have arisen as a result of the land-holding system in the country. Legislation governing land rights and ownership favoured the propertied class, and landlords and their agents did nothing for their tenants while extracting as much rent as they possibly could from them. Tenant farmers paid high rents, some had short one-year tenancies, after which they could be evicted at will, and they had little means to buy out their farmsteads.

At the same time, many farmers on long leases had agreed to pay rents which became more difficult to meet after the advent of what was later called the Long Depression. The latter was a worldwide economic slump that had a severe impact on the prices that could be achieved for agricultural products; it lasted from 1873 until 1879, but its effects continued to be felt into the 1890s. A farmer who could no longer pay his rent risked being subjected to eviction. This was carried out by men under the supervision of the Royal Irish Constabulary (RIC); in the event that a family barred their doors and refused to vacate their holding, their doors were wrenched open with crowbars and the roof would be smashed through in places, in order to make the house uninhabitable.

In response to such conditions, the Irish National Land League was formed in County Mayo in October 1879, and became a vigorous mass movement. One of its leaders was Michael Davitt, a long-time agitator for land reform and the rights of tenant farmers, while its unlikely first president was the charismatic Protestant landlord Charles Stewart Parnell, MP of County Wicklow. Its two initial aims were the reduction of excessive rents and the creation of a system that helped tenants to buy the lands that they worked. These aims developed into 'The Three F's': fair rent, free sale (whereby a tenant could sell his interest in the land to another tenant) and fixity of tenure (whereby a tenant could not be evicted as long as he paid his rent).

Meetings were held throughout the country to publicise the policies and practices of the Land League. In 1880, Puck Fair was deliberately chosen to be the location for the organisation's first ever meeting in Kerry, because it brought together people from the whole of the county.[16] At about four o'clock on the fair day itself, 'an immense crowd was addressed from the windows of a house in the Main-street'.[17] Timothy Harrington, owner of the *Kerry Sentinel*, first addressed the crowd (his speech summarised by a reporter from the newspaper):

That motto they had heard so frequently was 'The land of Ireland for the people of Ireland' (cheers). That short concise but telling phrase in which Michael Davitt gave expression to the National demand was but the simple assertion of the right of Irishmen to live on the land of their birth (loud cheers).

The story of Irish landlordism was no mere tradition amongst them. With all its diabolical machinery, with rack-rents and evictions, with the crowbar brigade, the famines and the emigrant ships, they were brought into contact. Every day the work of the crowbar was in operation in Kerry, and at the present moment they enjoyed the unenviable notoriety [of] standing at the head of the poll for evictions.[18]

Kerryman M.M. O'Sullivan, Assistant Secretary of the Land League organisation in Dublin, also spoke, and 'expressed his pleasure at having an opportunity of addressing the people of his native county':

In the West of Ireland, and other parts of Ireland as well, the tenant farmers had declared before Heaven that they would never pay a penny of rent pending legislation on the Land Question (cheers). He wanted to know today whether the people of Kerry would assist them in proclaiming that doctrine before the world (cheers). They had pledged the people to take no farm from which a tenant had been evicted; they had pledged them to give no aid in saving the crops on such a farm. If the landlord wished to save the crops he would bend his back himself and do one honest day's work (laughter and cheers). If he did not do so let the crops rot upon the ground, and let it be there as a waste before the world (cheers). In that way, and in that way only would they starve out Irish landlordism (cheers).

O'Sullivan asked the crowd to lift up their hands and pledge their agreement with the doctrines of the movement. They also passed a resolution agreeing to establish a branch of the Land League in Killorglin.

The RIC reported that the meeting 'was a noisy one owing to people having drink taken. They cheered and shouted for almost everything. There were a great number of people in town who took no part in the meeting'. [19] Although no branch of the League was formed in Killorglin, at the following year's fair the sentiments of the organisation influenced the presentation of the event, when 'mottoes, very uncomplimentary to landlordism, were everywhere conspicuously displayed'.[20]

Official attempts were made to resolve the land question with the Second Land Act of 1881, and judicial rent reviews were undertaken by a new

Land Commission. However, by 1882 the Land League became associated with acts of rural violence carried out by others (some in Kerry), its leading members were jailed, and a new 'No Rent' policy failed to be carried through. The organisation was suppressed, and in October 1882 Parnell founded a new body, the Irish National League, to campaign for Home Rule, the establishment of an Irish Parliament.

The Land Question continued into the late 1800s and early 1900s. In 1886, Fr Thomas Lawlor, parish priest of Killorglin, explained that, 'The judicial rents of a few years ago are rack rents now; for the prices of farm products since the judicial rents were fixed have fallen off 50 per cent'.[21] He added that about 1,000 notices of eviction had been served in the parish. Episodes of rural violence continued occasionally, some in the greater Killorglin area. The need to draft policemen to Puck Fair allowed roaming bands of men, known as Moonlighters, the opportunities of calling to houses in the wider neighbourhood to look for firearms, which could be used to fire shots at informants or members of the police.[22] After raiding houses, men were able to disperse by mingling with the crowds at the fair.[23]

PUCK FAIR AND THE NATIONAL QUESTION

The ultimate solution to Ireland's social and economic woes had long been suggested to be independence from the United Kingdom. After gaining control of the Irish Parliamentary Party (IPP), Parnell set about forcing the parliament in London to pay attention to Irish affairs, and attempted to advance the concept of Home Rule.

He marshalled popular support for the Parliamentary Party from the mass movement of the Irish National League. Over 1,000 branches of the League were founded across the country in 1885, including a branch in Killorglin, where its president was Fr Thomas Lawlor, a charismatic and able man.

The Home Rule movement foundered in 1890, after Captain William O'Shea initiated divorce proceedings against his wife, Kitty, citing Parnell as the other party involved. An explosion of moral outrage among the Irish public followed, Parnell was condemned, and the IPP split.

Although Fr Lawlor sided against the Parnellites after the Kitty O'Shea affair, the National Question and the Land Question continued to be supported at Puck Fair; an article on the event, published in 1894, cited the banners displayed there, which included, 'Home Rule! The Land for the People'.[24]

PUCK FAIR AND THE IRISH LANGUAGE

In 1893, Conradh na Gaeilge (the Gaelic League), an organisation dedicated to the preservation and promotion of the Irish language, was established by Douglas Hyde, of County Roscommon, and others. It was an apolitical organisation, but it naturally attracted many nationalist agitators, particularly as the spirit of the League was animated by Hyde's insistence on the necessity of de-Anglicising Ireland.

In Kerry, at the turn of the century, nearly half the population spoke Irish as well as English,[25] and some of the business of Puck Fair must have been conducted through the Irish language. A branch of the League was established in Killorglin by April 1901,[26] and Puck Fair that year went on to reflect some of its themes, with banners calling for 'Success to the Irish League', and supporting 'The Language and the Country'.[27] At the fair of

Traveller women and children on the street, 1954. (Inge Morath © The Inge Morath Foundation. Courtesy of Magnum Photos)

1908, the sunburst flag of Conradh na Gaeilge, known as An Gal Gréine, was among the flags displayed from the platform.[28]

Although its principal aim related to the Irish language, the Gaelic League's activities naturally flowed into support for other aspects of traditional Irish culture, and at the fair of 1909 it erected a platform where traditional musicians and dancers performed for the crowds.[29]

PUCK FAIR AND THE FIRST WORLD WAR

The outbreak of the First World War in July 1914 had an immediate impact on the fair. Horse traders received a boost that August, when buyers on behalf of the government attended and bought up many animals for service as army pack horses. In an effort to drive down prices, it was reported that a telegram was sent to officials, telling them to cease buying any more animals – with the intention that this information be circulated through the fair – but the horse dealers saw through the ruse, and continued to ask for high prices.[30] So many were sold that one train alone carried away fifteen wagons loaded with horses.[31]

During the war, many of the Traveller men, who had been members of the army reserves, were drafted into Irish regiments of the British Army, and as a result their numbers were said to be down at the fairs held for the duration.[32] Some of these men served with the Royal Munster Fusiliers, whose barracks was at Ballymullen, Tralee, and with the Royal Irish Rifles. Frank Wilson, a reporter with the *Press Agency*, approached a group of Traveller veterans at the fair field in 1934:

> Standing carelessly at the entrance, their backs to me, were three young men of the Sheridan clan apparently still in their thirties. Noticing that they had the Army clearly stamped on them, I said in a low quick voice from just behind them, 'Attention!' and quickly they jumped to position as if on parade. Taking out my cigarettes for them, 'Munsters, I suppose', I said. 'Munsters' the tallest of them said; 'Irish Rifles', said the other two. 'Let's have a talk over yonder', I said, and straightaway we became busy in a competitive recall of names and places and events. Mons, Namur, Liege, the Meuse, Cambria, Paschendale Ridge and many other places, remembered for their heat, passed in review.[33]

The fairs of the war years were prosperous ones for the farmers. Lady Edith Gordon wrote that the changes she had noticed were 'all for the better. Higher prices, less drink, less fighting'.[34] At the fair of 1915, the *Irish Times* reported that 'The attendance of buyers was large, and buying extremely brisk at exceptionally high prices'.[35] The fair of 1918, in the last year of the war, was busy, as reported in the *Kerryman*:

> From a business point of view, Puck, 1918, has created a new record. The supply in all departments was very good, the demand brisk, and the prices paid all round highly satisfactory. The railway returns provide, perhaps, the best record, especially when last year's figures are available … a total of 110 wagons of live stock, as against 60 last year.[36]

Lady Gordon felt that afterwards, however, 'the rush of the war, coming quickly, and bringing welcome profits, passed as quickly and left the town, as it left many others, with a shrinking trade'.[37]

Puck Fair and the Fight for Irish Freedom

Attempts by the Irish Parliamentary Party to achieve Home Rule for Ireland by constitutional means had failed at the British Parliament in 1886 and 1893, and as a result other political parties and groups formed in the aftermath.

Sinn Féin was established in 1905, and a Killorglin branch was set up in December 1907.[38] The local branch may have been responsible for a banner at the fair of 1908, 'Sinn Féin, Sinn Féin Amháin' (Ourselves, Ourselves alone),[39] although that slogan was also the motto of the Gaelic League, which had a branch in the town.

A third Home Rule Bill was finally passed by Parliament in London in 1914, but it was suspended from implementation by the outbreak of the First World War. By that time, a paramilitary force, the Irish Volunteers, had been founded to defend the concept of Home Rule, following the creation of the Ulster Volunteers, who were determined to resist it. The Irish Volunteers split after they were urged instead to fight on the continent for the cause of the British Empire; a smaller force of its members instead decided to stage a rebellion while Britain was distracted by the war with Germany.

The Volunteers, along with the explicitly revolutionary Irish Republican Brotherhood and socialist leader James Connolly's Irish Citizen Army, an armed force originally devised to protect striking workers from beatings by the police, assembled in Dublin on 24 April 1916 and took over various positions in the city centre. The Irish tricolour (of green, white and orange), a flag representing an independent Ireland, was hoisted aloft over the General Post Office in Sackville Street (later O'Connell Street) and fighting against the British Army began. A week later, the Irish forces had to surrender.

While the rebellion had no significant popular mandate beforehand, the execution of its leaders in May evoked a wave of public sympathy and anger. At Puck Fair later that year, 'a Sinn Féin flag' (the tricolour) was raised onto one of the poles of the goat stand as a mark of support for what had come to be called 'The Sinn Féin Rising'. Strictly speaking, the flag could not be flown as it was considered to be an illegal act under the Defence of the Realm Act of 1914, which forbade a number of petty activities for the duration of the war. In addition, not everyone in the town then supported the party or the rising, and the action 'was objected to by some parties'; a fight also broke out in the electricity station, which illuminated the stand, when the director of the light company turned off the lights, obscuring the flag.[40] Later that night, it was taken down by the police.[41]

At the fair of 1918, while three other flags appeared, the pole where the tricolour might be placed was left bare, '… so as it could not be hoisted its place was reserved and, like the empty benches in the House of Commons a short time ago,[42] its absence told its own tale. It surely was a very good idea and perhaps prevented conflict with the authorities, whose representatives – both militant and police – it might be said were present in great numbers'.[43]

The fair of 1920 was officially banned, but went ahead nonetheless.[44] The tricolour was flown from the goat platform, while the poles themselves were painted in the national colours.[45] The flag was again removed by the RIC, but a local woman, Mrs Nora Power, a publican and draper, came to the rescue, quickly stitching a new flag together, which three men then climbed the stand to restore.[46]

In order to bolster the forces of the RIC throughout Ireland, an auxiliary force had been recruited in Britain, whose improvised uniforms led to them being nicknamed the 'Black and Tans'. They were deployed between 1920 and 1921, and soon developed a notorious reputation for their hostile attitude towards the Irish, for the summary execution of combatants and civilians, and for the torching of a number of small towns. During the fair of 1920 one of these men shot the Puck goat. (Its skin was kept, and in 1958, American visitor Muriel Rukeyser was shown it and the bullet-hole.)[47]

In November 1920, in reprisal for the killing of two RIC men in Killorglin, the Black and Tans burnt out the Sinn Féin hall in Lower Bridge Street; beside it lay the rooms of the Total Abstinence Society, and the musical instruments belonging to the society were consumed in the flames.[48] The band, which had provided the musical accompaniment to the ceremonies of Puck Fair since 1908, was unable to carry on, and another local band was not formed until 1945.[49]

PUCK FAIR AND THE RED FLAG

Agitation to improve labourers' wages and conditions had been present in Kerry since at least 1915, when James Connolly had addressed a crowd of 3,000 people in Tralee in October, following which, branches of the Transport and General Workers Union were formed in the county.[50] In Killorglin, workers began to organise by spring 1920. The Killorglin correspondent of the *Kerryman* wrote in February:

'The appeal to farm labourers, men and women to organise is everywhere in evidence and, as far as we can see, is being well responded to ... The day of cheap labour is gone as is the day of bad treatment and cruelty for the maid servant.'[51] In March the agricultural labourers and household servants of the greater Killorglin area were reported to have come together and demanded, and been promised, better wages.[52] Cottiers organised, and twenty four of them successfully approached local farmers to get an additional acre to their garden plots.[53]

A formal branch of the TGWU was established in Killorglin by July 1920, the secretary of which was also a member of Sinn Féin:[54] those facts, and the recent agitation, may account for the presentation of flags at the Puck stand in August 1921, when antiquarian T.J. Westropp observed three Republican flags 'and one red one', the symbol of workers' rights and left-wing agitation. [55]

PUCK FAIR AND THE CIVIL WAR

Following the signing of the Anglo-Irish Treaty, after negotiations between Irish Republicans and the British in London in December 1921, the nationalist movement split between those who accepted the limited self-government offered by the treaty, and those for whom the agreement had not gone far enough. Pro- and Anti-Treaty forces prepared to fight each other, and outright military hostilities began in June 1922 and lasted until May 1923.

Killorglin was significantly involved in military operations between Free State and Republican forces in September 1922. Generally, hostilities in Kerry had made the holding of fairs throughout the county difficult, and from 3 August no train service had been available from Killorglin, which would have made the usual transport of cattle impossible.[56] There are no newspaper reports of Puck Fair in 1922, and it appears that it did not take place.

Notes

1 'Domestic News. Tralee, August 17', *Dublin Evening Post*, 26 August 1786.
2 Masses celebrated in people's homes.
3 Quoted in Kieran Foley, *History of Killorglin* (1988) page 34.
4 *Ibid.* page 44.
5 *Ibid.* page 48.
6 Kieran Foley, *History of Killorglin* (1988) page 49.
7 M.C.J., 'Puck Fair', *Tralee Chronicle*, 14 August 1847.
8 *Kerry Examiner*, 15 August 1848.
9 *Kerry Examiner*, 17 August 1849.
10 M.C.J., 'Puck Fair', *Tralee Chronicle*, 17 August 1850.
11 'Milltown, August 9, 1850, *Tralee Chronicle*, 17 August 1850.
12 'Dingle (From a Correspondent)', *Tralee Chronicle*, 17 August 1850.
13 'The Potato Crop', *Tralee Chronicle*, 16 August 1851.
14 'Puck Fair', *Tralee Chronicle*, 16 August 1851.
15 Kieran Foley, *History of Killorglin* (1988) page 53.
16 Donnacha Seán Lucey, *Land, Popular Politics and Agrarian Violence in Ireland: The Case of County Kerry, 1872-86* (University College Dublin Press, Dublin, 2011) page 59.
17 'The Land Agitation. Meeting in Killorglin', *Kerry Sentinel*, 13 August 1880.
18 *Ibid.*
19 Donnacha Seán Lucey, *Land, Popular Politics and Agrarian Violence in Ireland: The Case of County Kerry, 1872-86* (University College Dublin Press, Dublin, 2011) page 60.
20 'Puck Fair', *Kerry Sentinel*, 12 August 1881.
21 'How the Goats Saved Killorglin … Father Lawlor seeking aid for a Poverty-stricken People'. From the *Chicago Herald*. Reproduced in the *Kerry Sentinel*, 19 November 1886.
22 'Kerry Moonlighters', *Irish Times*, 13 August 1886.
23 *Ibid.*

24 M.C.K., 'Puck Fair', *The Irish Monthly*, Vol. 22, July 1894, page 374.

25 According to Thomas O'Donnell, MP. 'Killorglin Feis', *Freeman's Journal*, 12 December 1902.

26 'Connrad na Gaedilge. Executive Committee', *Freeman's Journal*, 5 April 1901.

27 'Puck Fair', *Kerry Sentinel*, 17 August 1901.

28 The press report called the flag 'the Rising Sun'. 'Pars from Puck', *Kerryman*, 15 August 1908.

29 'Pars From Puck', *Kerryman*, 21 August 1909.

30 'Puck Fair', *Kerry Sentinel*, 15 August 1914.

31 *Ibid.*

32 Kieran Foley, *History of Killorglin* (1988) page 107.

33 Frank Wilson, 'Fun and Sport in Kerry', *Kerry Reporter*, 11 August 1934.

34 Lady Gordon, *The Winds of Time* (John Murray, London, 1934) page 128.

35 '"Puck" Fair, Killorglin', *Irish Times*, 12 August 1915.

36 'The Fair', *Kerryman*, August 17, 1918.

37 'Killorglin, Then and Now', *Kerry Reporter*, 11 August 1934.

38 'Pars from Puck', *Kerryman*, 7 December 1907.

39 'Pars from Puck', *Kerryman*, 15 August 1908.

40 'A Midnight Scene at Puck. ... Fight in the Power House described at Petty sessions', *Kerryman*, 26 August 1916.

41 'The Irish Rebellion Flag at Puck', *Kerryman*, 19 August 1916.

42 Sinn Féin candidates elected in 1918 refused to sit in the British parliament.

43 'Pars from Puck', *Kerryman*, 17 August 1918.

44 Muriel Rukeyser, *The Orgy* (Andre Deutsch, London, 1965) page 142.

45 'Pars from Puck', *Kerryman*, 21 August 1920.

46 'Queen of Puck', *Kerryman*, 11 August 1989; 'Pa Houlihan's Puck Museum', *Kerryman*, 5 August 1983.

47 Muriel Rukeyser, *The Orgy* (Andre Deutsch, London, 1965) page 142.

48 Liam Foley, 'Killorglin', *Kerryman*, 11 December 1954; 'Pays the Rates', *Kerryman*, 6 August 1966.

49 'Killorglin', *Kerryman*, 18 August 1962.

50 Kieran McNulty, 'Revolutionary Movements in Kerry 1913 to 1923: A Social and Political Analysis', *Journal of the Kerry Archaeological and Historical Society*, Series 2, Vol. 1, 2001, pages 5-29.

51 'Pars from Puck', *Kerryman*, 28 February 1920.

52 'Pars from Puck', *Kerryman*, 6 March 1920.

53 'Pars from Puck', *Kerryman*, 27 March 1920.

54 'Pars from Puck', *Kerryman*, 22 March 1920; 'IT and GWU', *Kerryman*, 17 July 1920.

55 T.J.W., 'The Fair of Puck', *Journal of the Royal Society of Antiquaries of Ireland*, Sec. 6, Vol. X, 1921, page 182.

56 Tom Doyle, *The Civil War in Kerry* (Mercier, Dublin, 2008) pages 170 and 262.

4

PUCK FAIR AFTER IRISH INDEPENDENCE

The fairs that took place after the establishment of the Irish Free State in December 1922, were almost all deemed to be successful from the points of view of business and pleasure.[1] Attendances were good, and there was reportedly less fighting.[2] The only quibble was a noted decline in horse sales, which was attributed to the growing popularity of the motorcar.[3] A report of 1928 painted a picture of a vibrant event:

> Puck Fair, Kerry's great festive day … was held yesterday amidst characteristic scenes of joyful turmoil: and it was clearly evidenced that, unlike other Irish customs which have been strangled to death in the tentacles of war and emigration, the great annual event in the life of Killorglin has lost nothing of its historical glamour and traditional associations.
>
> Hundreds of hardy itinerants have tramped as many miles in the past few weeks to share in the joys and gains of Puck. Tinkers, pedlars, wandering minstrels and merchants of every description poured in from all points of the compass. They are concomitant with Puck Fair, an integral part of the great bazaar, and, in some respects, its dominating feature.
>
> On Sunday afternoon, after a special train from Tralee had discharged over 500 enthusiastic visitors, the streets presented a truly animated appearance. 'The town was open wide' with a vengeance. Each side of all the thoroughfares was lined with rival traders, hawkers, shooting galleries and wheels of fortune, while raucous ballad singers, solo, and in partnership added compound interest to a heterogeneous,

gay, discordant spectacle. The Killarney Pipers' band marched through the town for several hours, and, eventually halted beneath the lofty platform at the top of the sloping square where was witnessed the coronation of the Puck.[4]

A National Tone

The country having recently won its freedom, or a version of it, it is not surprising that the presentation of the fair went on to develop a more national tone. Throughout the 1920s and '30s there was a stress on the Irish language, Gaelic culture and Irish history. The banners that were hung about the town appear to have been displayed in the Irish language only. The fair of 1924 showed '*Tír gan teanga, tír gan anam*' (A land without its language is a land without its soul), as well as banners, in Irish, with 'Welcome to Puck Fair' and 'The king of the mountains forever'.[5] The fair of 1930 continued with other Irish slogans,[6] and while the banners of the interim years were not reported, there is no reason to imagine that they were any different. In 1932, the speech from the platform welcoming visitors was delivered in Irish, and a display of Irish dancing was performed.[7]

In 1935, there was a banner recalling the Ballykissane tragedy.[8] Irish Volunteers travelling by car, on a mission to do with the 1916 Rebellion, had taken a wrong turn in the dark and driven into the water off Ballykissane pier, Killorglin. Three men drowned, and their deaths represented the first casualties of the revolutionary period that followed.

When the opening ceremonies of Puck Fair were broadcast live by Radio Athlone (the precursor of Raidió Éireann) in 1936, local man William O'Brien gave the origins of the event as going back to Celtic times, before the arrival of the Viking and Norman invaders, and said of the presentation of the current ceremony that 'the settings of the Fair were Gaelic of the olden time. All the inscriptions were in the Irish language, and Irish-speaking Guards were on duty'.[9] The poster for the fair of 1938 claimed grandly that the fair had been the entertainment of some of the heroes of Irish mythology: 'This was the scene of Fionn's greatest episode and of many events in the lives of Diarmuid and Gráinne'.[10]

PUCK FAIR AND THE ECONOMIC WAR

The business done in 1930 marked the fair as 'the best for the past quarter of a century'.[11] In the next year, however, there was an outbreak of Foot and Mouth disease in Britain; Irish cattle were bought up by dealers for onward export there, and the outbreak of disease led to an embargo on the importation of any more animals into the country, meaning demand was slow and prices poor at the fair of 1931.[12] A long-term fall in demand for cattle followed as a consequence of the Economic War (1932-1938), a trade dispute between the governments of Ireland and Britain.

The trade war had been sparked by the refusal of Éamon de Valera's Fianna Fáil government to continue to pay back land annuities – the financial loans that Britain had established to enable Irish tenant farmers to buy out their farmsteads under the various Land Acts of the late nineteenth century and early twentieth century. Among the reasons for non-payment was the argument that:

> British landlords had no moral right to the land of Ireland in the first place. In de Valera's words, the lands to which the annuities related were 'rewards given in the past to military adventurers from England ... the British government has found it desirable to convert those land rewards into money, and it was manifestly unfair to ask the citizens of the Irish Free State, from whom the land had been taken, to pay compensation to the persons who had deprived them of it'.[13]

The British government, in an effort to recoup these lost revenues, imposed a 20 per cent import tax on Irish agricultural products. This had a severe affect, as up to 90 per cent of these were exported to Britain and demand, particularly for live cattle exports, collapsed.

The affect of the Economic War was felt immediately at the fair of 1932. 'Little Stock on Offer. Very Low Prices' was the headline in the *Kerry Reporter*. Puck Fair 'will have left behind it memoirs of disappointment from the business point of view', said the report.[14] Only eight wagons of cattle left Killorglin railway station, in contrast to the former average of over ninety.[15] The cattle trade at all fairs 'at first became alarmingly smaller and in a few months practically dried up altogether. The principal source of profit from the interior lands of these congested districts disappeared and the small holders, always poor, became poorer still'.[16]

There was a further knock-on affect on the local economy when labourers' purchasing power became diminished, as employment at agricultural work shrank and wages were said to have come down by 30 per cent.[17]

In 1935, in a move towards resolving the dispute, the government negotiated a deal with the British authorities – a 'Coal-Cattle Pact', whereby the government agreed to import more British coal in return for being permitted an increase of 30 per cent in the exports of cattle. The cattle business did not improve at first, when 'prices showed a slump'.[18] It seems the trade may have picked up in the following years, as no complaints were recorded, and in 1938, when the dispute was finally concluded, although sales of cattle were slow, 'most of the very large supply was disposed of at fairly satisfactory prices'.[19]

THE LIVESTOCK FAIR

While cattle sales had dropped during the 1930s, horse sales continued to hold up, and during that time, Puck Fair came to be described as mainly a horse fair.[20] Although horses had also been subject to the British export tariff, demand for them appears to have been strong enough from within the domestic economy.

A quiet chat, 1980. (© Martin Parr. Courtesy of Magnum Photos)

No sale, 1954. (Inge Morath © The Inge Morath Foundation. Courtesy of Magnum Photos)

The Kerry Cow was still offered for sale from the 1920s to the '40s, although their numbers varied wildly; in 1928, only 15 animals were presented, as opposed to 150 to 200 in former years, yet the following year the breed was said to have predominated over others.[21] In 1941, they were still observed at the fair.[22]

Most of the cattle dealers who attended were from Northern Ireland. In 1950 English travel writer Stowers Johnson met a couple of them, whom he found evasive about their business and scornful of southerners.[23] He believed that they were buying cattle cheaply and afterwards selling them on at a high profit, seemingly in the Irish midlands, Northern Ireland or Britain.[24]

VISITORS LOVE PUCK FAIR

While the business side of the fair had been troubled for a time, the social and tourist aspect, in contrast, prospered, and the numbers of people attending the event went from strength to strength. Irish-Americans began arriving at the fair by 1930 and were noted visitors throughout the decade.[25] Visitors came also from England, often attracted by accounts of the great fishing to be had in Kerry,[26] and Irish sightseers came from as far away as Dublin.[27] The increasing popularity of the motorcar in the 1930s allowed those who could afford them to travel to the fair, while that decade's craze for the pleasures of the great outdoors brought urban hikers too.[28] By 1937, attendance was estimated to be 25,000.[29]

Some of the visitors were accommodated in the town's several hotels. The Railway Hotel remained popular; there was an establishment called Taylor's Hotel, which operated from the 1920s to the '40s, seemingly at Lower Bridge Street;[30] there was the Laune Hotel (now The Bianconi), which stood at the corner of Lower Bridge Street and Annadale Road, which also operated from the 1920s until the '40s;[31] and the former Ventry Arms, afterwards known as the Commercial Hotel, remained open until the 1950s.[32] Many private houses in the town were also converted into temporary guesthouses, although in 1940, 'despite all the efforts of the residents many were compelled to snatch a few hours' sleep in their cars'.[33] Generally, those who could not find a place to stay in the town travelled to outlying villages such as Milltown and Glenbeigh.[34]

THE COMMITTEE

After the demise of the Total Abstinence Society in 1920, the role of organising the public aspects and entertainments of the fair was taken over by a formal Puck Fair committee[35] (and successive committees have continued to organise the spectacle of the fair to this day). The committee began to produce posters advertising the fair ('The origin of which is lost in the mists of antiquity')[36] and, afterwards, official timetables for the event.[37] They also introduced other activities to entertain the crowds during the three days, such as regattas and motorboat races on the Laune.[38]

The local branch of the Gaelic League continued to have a part in the presentation of the event. During the 1930s there were traditional singing and dancing competitions in association with the League,[39] while the Irish banners and nationalist slogans were probably supplied by the organisation.

The business side of the fair remained within the purview of the Foley family, with Thomas T. Foley collecting tolls for the animals sold during these decades.[40] Patrick Houlihan later quoted the various charges due, from a toll sheet of the 1920s: 'Horses 10*d* – Cows 6*d* – Bullocks and Heifers 4*d* – Sheep and Lambs 1*d* – Asses 4*d* – Goats 1*d* – Pigs 3*d*'.[41]

In 1926, the 6th Baron Ventry, Arthur William Eveleigh-de Moleyns, sold off his estate to the Irish Land Commission; his property included the fair field, but this did not affect the running of the livestock sales. (The Commission later sold the field to a member of the Puck Fair committee, Patrick 'Duffy' O'Shea, in 1959.)[42]

Michael Houlihan still had the job of erecting the goat platform and manoeuvring the goat cage onto the top of it.[43] He was also charged with feeding the animal for the duration (usually with cabbages and water).[44] By 1936, he had converted the old two-stage platform into a three-stage one, whereby a band played on the bottom tier, Irish dancers could be seen performing on the middle tier and the goat occupied the top tier.[45] Each tier was reached by a ladder from the level below. Flags flew from the poles, usually including the tricolour and the Stars and Stripes,[46] while at night the whole platform was illuminated by multi-coloured electric bulbs.[47]

Milking time, 1954. (Inge Morath ©The Inge Morath Foundation. Courtesy of Magnum Photos)

PUCK AND THE WAR

Puck Fair carried on as normal during the Second World War (1939-1945). The fair of 1941 was advertised happily as 'strictly neutral and still surviving wars, threats of invasion and political world upheaval'.[48] Generally, the fairs of the war years were thronged with Irish crowds.[49] The fair of 1942 was afterwards said to have attracted a record attendance, and that of 1945 was described as one of the best for years.[50]

Visitor Muriel Rukeyser was later told that there had been a black market at Puck Fair during the war, but she was given no details.[51] Items such as food and fuel were rationed in Ireland during what was euphemistically termed The Emergency. The biggest shortages for country households were tea, sugar, cigarettes and tobacco; there was also a lack of inner tubes for bicycle tyres, which was a significant issue in a rural society that relied so much upon such transport. Some smugglers and even day-trippers plied a lucrative trade from Northern Ireland into the Republic in the early years of the war, and this may have been a source of contraband goods, at first- or second-hand.[52]

Foreign visitors returned after the war, so that – added to Irish sightseers – a remarkable 50,000 people were reported as attending the fair in 1947.[53]

TRAVELLERS (AND GYPSIES)

Sightseers had plenty to entertain them at the fairs during the decades of the 1930s and '40s. Travellers set up games of chance, and presented exotic diversions:

> One exploits three thimbles, under one of which is concealed a most elusive pea. A boy from Cromane made two valiant attempts to locate it in vain. But he was a youthful sportsman, and paid his two shillings with a smile. There are roulette tables in abundance. A small boy entreats visitors to view the world's smallest bull, only 26 inches high ... Across the road is a booth in which is kept a cow with two mouths; scrawled in uncouth letters upon a placard, the visitor is informed he may see the phenomenon for the small figure of 3*d*.[54]

Bird's Amusements and traditional caravans in the fair field, 1954. (Inge Morath © The Inge Morath Foundation. Courtesy of Magnum Photos)

As they had done for years, the Travellers arrived two weeks early for Puck. By 1934 some of them came in cars and vans, although they also continued to use traditional caravans.[55] Among the families gathered were the Sheridans, from Rathkeale, County Limerick, whose patriarch, Dan Sheridan, was known as the 'King of the Horse Traders', and who was photographed at Puck by the celebrated Fr Browne.[56] There were also the Coffeys from Kerry, Wards from the west of Ireland, and the Reillys from Tipperary, as well as families who had come from as far away as Dublin.[57]

During the 1930s, some of the Travellers gathered at the fair field, privately. 'It was, I learned from the bystanders, a "Tinkers' Fair", convened by themselves and attended and used only by them for barter and sale purposes', wrote journalist Frank Wilson.[58] Holding their own fair in parallel with the official fairs of Ireland was sometimes a feature of Travellers' engagement with these events; at the harvest fair of Ballyshannon in County Donegal, for example, they held their own fair the day following.[59] At Puck Fair, holding their event early allowed them to sell animals without incurring the tolls levied during the fair proper.[60]

The Travellers generally parked along by the far side of the Laune River. A visitor walked over early one morning in 1930 to have a look at their encampment:

81

Temporary sleeping tents were erected beside the carts, and I came upon
one that was evidently too small to accommodate the full length of the
'man of the house', for his feet extended from under that portion of the
canvas which formed the foot of the tent. I shall never forget the soles of
those feet. They shone in the light of the morning sun as if they had been
coated with black enamel. Outside another tent, a woman was holding a
baby in one arm while the fingers of the other hand were curled about the
bowl of a blackened clay pipe.[61]

In contrast, Cork writer Robert Gibbings described a Traveller wedding
party held in Killorglin, in the open air, the week after the fair of 1949:

'No hotel in Ireland would have more elegant tables', I was told afterwards.
'You never saw the like of them, spread along the road among the caravans,
with all the silver and the linen cloths and the jellies and the cutlery and
the cakes and the hams – a power of money was spent on it all. And the
drapers' shops was nearly sold out with all the clothes that were bought.
The bride had on her a dress of blue, and every man was in his best, and
the women with bright shawls, and handkerchiefs on their heads.'

That evening four barrels of stout stood on the parapet of the bridge,
three on one side for the men and one on the other for the women, 'for
everything was very orderly.' And the bride's father sat outside his caravan
inviting all the passers-by to come in for a whiskey or sherry or port, and
there was the grandest singing and dancing all night.[62]

Visitor Stowers Johnson felt that there was a kind of social distinction
between the Travellers. There were a small number, who were involved in
the cattle trade and who had motor caravans; they parked with the wood-
and-canvas caravans on the far side of the river along the Killarney road.
A poorer element, which had only carts and tents with them, gathered along
the road to Kilgobnet, on the town side of the river.[63]

While Travellers were sometimes referred to as 'gypsies', in light of their
canvas-covered caravans and nomadic lifestyle, Romany gypsies, as such,
seem to have appeared at Puck Fair during the 1930s and '40s.[64] They are
first mentioned in an anonymous poem about the fair, published in the
Kerry Reporter in 1934, in which they are distinguished from the Travellers:

The back of a Traveller caravan, 1972. (© Josef Koudelka, Courtesy of Magnum Photos)

It would not be 'Puck' if the tinkers
Were not there in some meddlesome way.

It's a hunting-ground, too, for the gipsy,
What a picturesque strange living set!
Your future to them is no mystery,
If you've silver enough for their net.[65]

The fair of 1935 included 'gypsies, with their gaily coloured wagons and their friends in less polite beggary, the tinkers'.[66] In 1944, Ulster writer and film-maker Richard Hayward went to the far side of the bridge, where he saw 'the caravans of the gypsies and the distinct and smaller portable habitations of the tinkers'.[67]

Gypsies seem to have travelled to Ireland from Britain, although why they appeared is unclear; it is possible that they met Irish Travellers who frequented fairs in England, such as Appleby Fair in Cumbria and Epsom Fair in Surrey, and decided to travel by ferry over to Ireland to seek out the Irish fairs. They may have remained here during the war to avoid the difficulties posed by a society on a war footing, or the prospect of military service; after the war they must have returned to England, as they are no longer mentioned in relation to Puck Fair. Evidence of their general presence in Ireland comes as a result of their encounters with the police or the courts: in 1932, Fred and George Gentle, 'who belonged to a party of gypsies had their caravans obstructing people passing along the road' in County Tipperary;[68] a year later, gypsies fought police at Omagh as they tried to arrest them, rescuing some of their number but leaving one George Gaskins;[69] in County Galway in 1939, gypsy Andrew Price was arrested;[70] and in 1944, the *Connacht Tribune* reported that 'Two gypsies named Thomas and Carolina Smyth' were acquitted of unlawful possession of three donkeys.[71]

Traditionally, Romany women made their living as fortune-tellers. Those skills, or the semblance of them, appear to have been acquired in turn by the Traveller women, so that by 1941 they were offering to read young countrymen's palms.[72] Stowers Johnson later observed that some of the fortune-tellers gathered at the bridge, or at Lower Bridge Street, while others made their way to the railway station at Iveragh Road, to encounter passengers from each train that arrived.[73]

Amusement Parks and Fairground Games

During the 1920s, Tierney's Amusements appeared at Puck Fair, although little is remembered about them beyond the name.[74] By the 1930s, two different amusements shows pitched up at the fair. One was habitually camped at the edge of the fair field, while the other seems to have been sited somewhere on Iveragh Road. These housed tables with various games, such as roulette, as well as traditional fairground attractions, such as merry-go-rounds and swing-boats, and blared their existence to the world with two loud organs.[75] One of them was apparently Williams' Amusements;[76] the other was Piper's Amusements, which travelled throughout Kerry and Cork during the 1930s. Piper's was joined, and replaced, by Bird's Amusements, which arrived in Kerry for the first time in 1940 – this went on to provide entertainment at Puck Fair for many decades.[77] (Piper's went on to use their experience of Killorglin's event to have re-enactments of the Puck Fair ceremony performed in towns across County Cork, such as Bandon, Ballineen and Bantry, during the 1940s; these included a parade, and the crowning of a decorated goat, which was then placed on a raised platform.)[78]

Stalls on the street also offered traditional fairground games. One involved a player trying to pass a metal hoop all the way along a zigzag wire attached to a large battery (probably an old car battery). Played elsewhere, if the hoop and the wire were touched together, a buzzer would sound, but the primitive version at Puck Fair appears to have meant that the player got a small electric shock; 'Happy children … "try their nerves" for tuppence on an ancient electric battery which nearly paralysed you'.[79]

Another game involved a player trying to win cheap prizes by throwing a ring around them. (This seems to have been the game known as 'Hoopla'.)[80] A visitor recalled: 'On my mantelpiece I have enshrined a curious ornament, or rather atrocity, which was presented to me by a loud-voiced lady after I had encircled it with a wooden hoop thrown from a distance. It is fashioned of china and is supposed to represent some form of animal life'.[81]

Not only prizes but also the general range of goods sold by the travelling stallholders were reckoned to be of poor quality. According to the *Kerry Reporter*, purchasers 'soon discover all that glitters is not gold. Indeed, after close examination of the articles of all kinds sold on the streets, anyone of intelligence can see they are never value for the money paid'.[82]

Kick-the-Ball, 1954. (Inge Morath © The Inge Morath Foundation. Courtesy of Magnum Photos)

Although it was not often observed, the established shopkeepers of Killorglin may have resented the arrival of the street-traders at Puck, probably fearing a consequent loss of business. 'I must remark … that traders of all kinds have a really big grievance in the way that a lot of [them] appear at Puck Fair, and such places to sell goods on the streets', declared a reporter.[83]

DANCING, MUSIC AND SONG

From the 1920s, all-night dances took place at the Carnegie Hall on Market Road,[84] and, from the late 1930s, there were dances at the Oisin Ballroom, Iveragh Road.[85] From 1948, the Oisin was joined on the same street by Lyons' Ballroom.[86] In 1940, the Laune Ballroom was opened on Lower Bridge Street, but it does not appear to have functioned for long.[87] These venues presented small bands playing music-hall songs, or small orchestras playing dance music.[88] The biggest hall was the Oisin, owned by Patrick 'Duffy' O'Shea, which could accommodate up to 2,000 people and boasted extensive facilities inside, such as bars, a café, ice-cream parlours, and card rooms; it had a sprung floor, perfect for dancing, and described itself as 'Just the place to have your fling/ Where fun is yours and swing is king'.[89]

Stowers Johnson noted that the dancing at Puck Fair was the talk of the town among the young women for weeks beforehand. He took an early morning tour of the halls, thinking that he might hear some Irish music, but instead found waltzes, foxtrots and sambas:

At the doors a motley crowd was gathered, adolescents and rustics, young and old, taking up the pavement and blocking the roadway, some content to listen to the music, others pushing hard to peep at the dancing, perhaps feeling too shy or too uncouth to go in and take the floor.

Young fellows of about twenty-five years surrounded me to ask for my 'pass-out'. If I were going home they would be very grateful: they had lost theirs and could not get in. Without question I surrendered it and slipped away not looking back nor bothering more, but afterwards I learned that all the dances became rougher and coarser as the morning came because of all these somewhat disreputable 'pass-outs' who passed in![90]

Floor space in pubs was also allocated for less formal dancing from nine in the evening until four in the morning.[91]

Traditional singers and musicians played in the crowded pubs, as visitor Garry Hogg recorded:

> I have said that there was not a square foot of space unoccupied. Yet I heard music, and sure enough there were two fiddlers, a youngster and an older man, fiddling for dear life among all that press … The two men seemed actuated by one mind, for as one played the other tucked his fiddle beneath his arm and thrust a greasy cap beneath the nose of anyone within immediate reach. Though they might be separated, the two of them, by several yards, so soon as one player desisted the other picked up the very note and beat that followed, while the first would off with his cap and collect from the drinkers at his elbow. There was never a note missed, a beat dropped.[92]

In 1945, Roger McHugh, of the English Department at University College Dublin, heard a Traveller singing 'The Galbally Farmer', about an agricultural labourer who is hired by a mean farmer; a ballad which has up to twenty-one verses. 'He sang it slowly, deliberately shaping the words, drawing some of them out and running them into the next for emphasis, with many turns and half-turns in the tune.'

> I remember it well, t'was a cold Christmas night
> To a hearty good supper he did me invite
> To a sup of sour milk that would physic a snipe
> And give you the trotting disorder.
>
> The wet ould potatoes would poison the cats
> The barn where my bed was swarming with rats
> The fleas in my belly were big and were fat
> I spent the night scratching till morning.

'A pint for the singer!' somebody shouted out afterwards.[93]

Traditional music was also played in the streets. A journalist in 1938 was transfixed by a melodeon player outside a pub on Gathering Day:

'No notation known to musical science could do justice to such subtlety of intonation, such wild, unconventional beauty'.[94] Ballads continued to be sung, with the tale of 'The Dingle Puck Goat' becoming a regular and most suitable public performance:[95]

> I am a young jobber both foolish and airy,
> The green hills of Kerry I came for to see;
> I went back to Dingle to buy up some cattle;
> I hope you will listen to what happened to me.
>
> I entered the Fair of a Saturday morning
> And the first thing I saw was a long-legged goat.
> Bedad then, says I, I'm now to commence dealing
> I think, my old hero, you're worth a pound note.

It was explained to Stowers Johnson that each ballad singer sang only one ballad throughout the days of the fair. This may have been so that the good singers could be identified and enable members of the public to catch up with them at any time, maybe to supply them with a few coins when they found that they had them after an animal sale or a few drinks. Johnson found only one street singer during his stay at the fair of 1950, John Wilson, who accompanied himself on the accordion to sing 'The Ballad of the Battle of Knockanure', a song which commemorated three young men who had been detained and shot by the Black and Tans in north Kerry in 1921. The daughter of the owner of the Railway Hotel on Iveragh Road, where Stowers Johnson was staying, noticed that this was the first fair where the words were not being offered for sale on printed sheets, and she thought it a bad sign about the health of the tradition. She herself sang 'The Bard of Armagh' and 'Green the Rushes O' one day at the hotel. Johnson also heard a young lad in the hotel bar performing 'The Flower of Sweet Strabane'.[96]

The advent of the record player added yet more music to the fair. One reporter found, 'booths proclaiming their business with the assistance of a gramophone. I stop for a moment listening to a gramophone record of an Irish ballad, new to me. As I listen the air is confused with other songs, and an old lady of the gypsy type marks the time with her head and dances a few bars'.[97]

PUCK FOOD

Food and confectionery continued to be sold to visitors at stalls on the streets, at restaurants, and in private houses.[98] 'In the matter of feeding so great a multitude, Killorglin rises nobly to the occasion, and what are on all other days of the year ordinary private houses become temporary restaurants bedecked with bunting and advertisements offering meals of every description at reasonable prices'.[99]

A particular offering at Puck Fair was mutton pies in soup; a woman who had lived in Killorglin as a young girl in the 1930s recalled an old lady called Mary who had an eating house in the town: 'I must have made a million trips to Mary's during Puck. I brought a soup plate, into which she put the pie and poured on the soup. As I was an only child, I could carry only one at a time – hence the number of trips … As far as I remember, Mary charged fourpence for the pies'.[100]

The lady also sold another Puck Fair speciality, 'crubeens', boiled pigs feet wrapped in newspaper.[101] 'As they oozed fat, it was quite a feat getting

Upper Bridge Street, with the Commercial Hotel to the left, *c.* 1900. (From the Lawrence Collection. Courtesy of the National Library of Ireland)

them home before the paper pulped. Often I didn't'. Crubeens were soft and tender and had a salty, bacon flavour. They were sold as a snack and remained hugely popular at Puck Fair well into the 1960s.[102]

Ice cream was also a favourite. Stowers Johnson saw that 'Between the Railway Station and the Fair there were ice-cream bars by the dozen. What a sight it was, these hordes of country folk moving slowly forward past the tramps, beggars and the pestering gypsies, licking their wafers and cornets!'[103]

Some stalls sold nothing but sweet treats. 'Along the sides of the streets, carts covered with awnings of canvas are turned into temporary shops which are stocked with such delicacies as gingerbreads, coloured sugar-sticks, etc., all in tempting array.'[104]

Puck Drink

During the fair, Killorglin's pubs stayed open for three days.[105] They were granted exemption orders to enable them to serve alcohol almost continuously, except for a break between 1 a.m. and 2 a.m. – a break that was usually ignored. The famous American pictorial magazine, *LIFE*, visited the fair in 1941, where it found the drinking 'continuous and boisterous', while the streets were 'lined with countrymen so drunk they cannot move'.[106] Garry Hogg noted that:

> … bedraggled women stood behind the bar counters, bleary-eyed, tousle-headed, half-asleep, still mechanically opening bottles for the men who lounged against the counters or sprawled on the wooden benches put there for the use of those who could no longer stand. I saw more drunk men in ten yards than I have seen elsewhere in the past ten years: not fighting drunk, I have to admit; they had probably reached and passed that stage round about midnight and were now in the maudlin state, slobbering as they spoke, spilling the beer if they were foolish enough to be trying to drink it by the glass, clumsily reaching for their own lips with bottle-necks, like impatient babies at the breast.

The writer Seán O'Faolain visited the fair in the late 1930s, where he saw '… two men, so mouldy with drink that they could not stand, swaying opposite one another, the head of one approaching the head of the other, which would just then sway the other way. Suddenly one of them bit the lobe of the ear of the other in a wild snap when he got near enough'.[107]

Garry Hogg marvelled that drink was not only served in pubs; men could stand and drink whisky or bottles of Guinness in the town's butchers, grocers, newsagents, chemists and hardware merchants.

Not everyone accepted that drinking was a defining feature of the event, however. A Mr McGillicuddy of Massachusetts fumed:

> I was born in the town of Killorglin and can still see my name on the door in your picture of Puck Fair. I have never seen the people lying in the streets drunk. I have never seen the fighting, gambling, etc. which your magazine depicts of life at Puck Fair.[108]

A telegram of protest was sent to *LIFE* magazine by Mr Mulvihill, a Kerryman of the fraternal Irish-American organisation, the Ancient Order of Hibernians, who demanded a retraction, complaining that the article and the 'accompanying pictures of pigs, alleged inebriates, crooked gamblers, horse-traders and thieves' encouraged racial prejudice against the Irish.[109]

The prospect of three days of non-stop drinking appealed very much to Welsh poet Dylan Thomas. In 1946 he persuaded the *London Picture Post* to let him have £50 as an advance for a proposed article about Puck Fair.[110] He and his wife, Caitlin, and their friends, Bill and Helen McAlpine, then travelled to Killorglin, where both men declared that they were simply going to drink continuously for the duration. Accordingly, they planted themselves at the counter of one of the bars and stood there drinking Guinness and talking for two days and two nights, until finally they were so drunk they were unable to speak. On the morning of the third day they had become completely comatose and had to be thrown into the back of a lorry and deposited back at their lodgings.[111] The proposed article was never written.

A BELT OF THE CROZIER

A three-day event consisting, for many, of three days of drinking, and the enthronement of a goat upon a public stage seems to have survived for a significant number of years without receiving 'a belt of the crozier' – condemnation from the Catholic hierarchy. Perhaps disapproval was implied: the ubiquitous appearance of a priest on any local committee in rural Ireland is entirely absent from every Puck Fair committee that ever was. In 1945, however, Killorglin parish priest Fr Daniel Finucane declared that he wished to see an end to the fair,[112] and the Dean of Kerry, Monsignor Donal Reidy, agreed, describing the event sharply as 'The growth of a modern legend from the surmises of folklorists – a rural sarcasm at a wretched fair in a once-wretched town'.[113] Two years later, there was an attempt by the clergy and some locals to get the organising committee to replace the goat parade with a religious pageant, and to substitute the goat with a religious icon.[114] That idea was successfully rejected and Puck Fair carried on as it was.

The first appearance of clerical condemnation of the fair in the 1940s may have been related to the commencement of international media attention directed towards it. By the 1930s and '40s, Puck Fair had ceased to be simply an attraction for the people of Killorglin, its extensive hinterland, and Kerry as a whole. It had become an object of national, and then international, attention via a developing media. British and American newspapers and magazines began to flock to Puck Fair during the 1940s. Newsreel company British Movietone News visited the fair of 1933, making *'Puck Fair' is Held in County Kerry*, and returned in 1935 to film *Puck Fair at Killorglin*.[115] It may have been tolerable for the wild event to have passed for years in local and national legend, but the rise of outside attention threatened to alter the impression of a calm, clean and wholesome Ireland that both the Catholic Church and the State wished to convey to the world, following the establishment of the Irish republic.

THE GOAT CEREMONY

Like many traditional folk customs that appear fixed and immutable, the goat ceremony retained older elements, while also continuing to change and develop: the scene that was witnessed in the 1940s was different in many respects from that which was seen in the 1840s. (This process continued into the following decades and up to the present day.)

From the late 1920s, the goat in his cage was carried along on a modern lorry, provided by Foley's garage of Lower Bridge Street, which had been decorated and styled as the royal coach, preceded by a group of costumed boys mounted on ponies.[116] A further group of young boys acted as a guard of honour, surrounding the goat. A report from 1928 stated that before the parade arrived, 'a scout will announce in the town that "the king is coming".'[117] In 1936, the riders were described as 'dressed in green and gold';[118] in later decades boys or young men were dressed to represent members of the mythological band of warriors the Fianna, and that may have been the intention here, given the emphasis on Irish history and culture during this period.

The parade began at the bridge or, from the mid-1930s, outside the recently built houses of Baile Nua, on the far side of the Laune River.[119] Richard Hayward observed the start of the fair in 1944:

And then the fun began ... the music of fiddles and melodeons came from the far edge of the town – a sudden silence fell upon the crowd and one could actually feel that they were all listening to those distant strains – and then came something between a great corporate sigh and the sound the wind makes when it sweeps over the top of a fine crop of standing wheat – and with that babel broke lose. A line of six fiddlers, playing finely like one man and with a terrific sense of rhythm, started the Derry hornpipe, and a great fat fellow, 'with drink taken', came from somewhere nearby and broke into the dance with much skill and spirit; but too much spirit of the one kind, for as the crowd widened out to make a circle round the musicians and the dancer, the poor fellow stumbled and fell flat on his back. He was a very big man, as I have said, but before the roar of laughter broke out to greet his discomfiture, he was on his feet again like a cat and into the dance for all he was worth. A great cheer broke out at this, for they are sporting people these Kerry farmers, and I must admit I added my own voice to theirs.[120]

During the 1920s and '30s the parades had been accompanied by the Killarney Pipers' band and the Tralee Boy Scouts band, which played from 1936.[121] Tunes played during the 1940s included 'The Kerry

Dance', 'The Rose of Tralee', and 'The Harvest Home',[122] as well as 'The Minstrel Boy' and 'The Wearing of the Green'.[123] Both bands included in their repertoire the song 'Long Live King Puck', which had first been played by the local band of the Total Abstinence Society in 1908.[124] From 1945 until the 1960s, Killorglin once again had its own band in the form of the Laune Pipers.[125]

A CROWN AND A QUEEN

There were two important developments introduced to the goat ceremony during the decades following Irish independence. The first was that the goat was no longer simply hoisted up and enthroned – now he was crowned. Initially, the crown was made of cardboard.[126] By 1952 it had become a fancier one made of metal,[127] probably the copper crown seen in 1955.[128] Crowning the animal may have been done in earlier years, but it was not mentioned before 1928.[129] Newsreel footage from 1935 showed a man doing the honours; in 1944 it was done by a boy 'courtier'; and in the following year by a man who also read out a proclamation of welcome in Irish.[130]

From at least 1949, however, there was a girl-queen to do the task, and this development became a central feature of the goat ceremony ever afterwards. The notion of a queen may have been inspired by the story that the mythological Queen Scotia (supposedly one of the leaders of the Milesians, one of the ancient races of Ireland) had passed through Puck Fair;[131] in 1951, an account of the origins of the fair quoted an old man who recited part of a poem, which he had heard as a boy:

A Milesian Queen coming to see
Puck Fair, died in Gleann Scothaidhe,
Diarmuid and Grainne and Fionn the Bold,
Joined in the revels in the days of old.[132]

The role of the Queen of Puck Fair would become one of the most prominent features of the event as the years went on, and, in modern times, photographs of the horned goat with the robed girl-queen became emblematic of

The 'Queen of Puck' crowns the goat, 1973. (© The Kennelly Archive)

the whole affair. Of course, this means that one of the scenes of the fair that has contributed to the suspicions of various observers that the ceremony must be quite ancient and pagan, was in fact a modern introduction.

In 1949, Robert Gibbings watched:

... as the strains of the pipes were heard returning to the square, the dancing ceased and a table draped in green was moved into the centre of the stage. On the table was a golden crown. A young girl wearing a silver crown and the purple mantle of a queen took her place beside it. Now a momentary hush fell on the assembly as the procession halted and the pipes ceased their chanting. In contrast to the young folk, hitherto most in evidence, strong men came forward and lifted Puck and his throne from the lorry to the stage awaiting him. Then with the national colours held high, with onlookers standing to attention, and the pipes playing The Dawning of the Day, the queen placed the golden crown on the goat's head.[133]

PUCK FAIR THRIVES BUT KILLORGLIN FADES

From the 1920s to the '40s, Puck Fair seems to have been successful, apart from the duration of the tariff war. Not only did the farmers and street-sellers thrive, as they generally did, but the town itself did well out of the event: the pubs, as always, but with the rise in visitor numbers, the town-dwellers were also able to earn money running temporary guesthouses and eateries.

But what of Killorglin beyond Puck Fair? Local man Liam Foley observed, in 1945, 'The weekly market ... shows how the business of Killorglin has gone down in recent years'.[134] Killorglin was hugely popular for three days in August, but for the rest of the year, it seems, the town was quiet.[135]

Notes

1 *Kerry Reporter*, 25 August 1928.
2 'At the Fair of Puck', *Kerry Reporter*, 18 August 1928.
3 *Kerry Reporter*, August 16, 1924; *Kerry Reporter*, 25 August 1928.
4 'At the Fair of Puck', *Kerry Reporter*, 18 August 1928.
5 *Kerry Reporter*, 16 August 1924.
6 'Puck Fair', *Kerry Reporter*, 16 August 1930.
7 'Puck Fair', *Kerry Reporter*, 13 August 1932.
8 'Kerry's Great Harvest Fair and Carnival', *Kerryman*, 17 August 1935.
9 'Puck Fair at Killorglin', *Irish Independent*, 11 August 1936.
10 Quoted in 'The Festival of Puck', *Irish Independent*, 13 August 1938.
11 'Puck Fair', *Kerry Reporter*, 16 August 1930.
12 'Puck Fair, Killorglin', *Kerryman*, 15 August 1931.
13 Donal Ó Drisceoil, 'When Dev Defaulted: The Land Annuities Dispute, 1926-38', www.historyireland.com.

14 'Puck Fair', *Kerry Reporter*, 13 August 1932.

15 'Puck Fair Failure', *Irish Times*, 13 August 1932.

16 'Killorglin, Then and Now', *Kerry Reporter*, 11 August 1934.

17 *Ibid.*

18 'Kerry's Great Harvest Fair and Carnival', *Kerryman*, 17 August 1935.

19 'Puck Fair Crowds', *Irish Independent*, 12 August 1938.

20 'Kerry's Great Harvest Fair and Carnival', *Kerryman*, 17 August 1935.

21 'At the Fair of Puck', *Kerry Reporter*, 18 August 1928; *Kerry Reporter*, 17 August 1929.

22 Rodney Gallop, 'Puck Fair at Killorglin', *Geographical Magazine*, August 1942, page 194.

23 Stowers Johnson, *Before And After Puck* (Fortune Press, London, 1953) pages 77 and 122.

24 *Ibid.* pages 78 and 123.

25 Puck Fair', *Kerry Reporter*, 16 August 1930; 'Kerry's Great Harvest Fair and Carnival', *Kerryman*, 17 August 1935; 'Puck Fair Crowds', *Irish Independent*, 12 August 1938.

26 Frank Wilson, 'Fun and Sport in Kerry', *Kerry Reporter*, 11 August 1934.

27 'Puck Fair Crowds', *Irish Independent*, 12 August 1938.

28 'Kerry's Great Harvest Fair and Carnival', *Kerryman*, 17 August 1935.

29 'All the Fun of Puck Fair', *Irish Independent*, 11 August 1937.

30 'Larceny of Motor Car', *Kerryman*, 18 April 1925; 'Vacancies for Girls', *Kerryman*, 28 June 1947; Patrick Houlihan, *Cast a Laune Shadow: Reminiscences of Life in Killorglin* (1997) page 47.

31 Advertisement, *Kerryman*, 29 June 1929; advertisement, *Kerryman*, 11 August 1945.

32 Advertisement by Commercial Hotel, Killorglin, *Kerryman*, 10 July 1954.

33 'Killorglin Crowded for Puck Fair', *Kerryman*, 17 August 1940.

34 'Killorglin's "King" is Crowned', *Irish Independent*, 11 August 1943; 'Thousands of Visitors at Puck Fair', *Irish Press*, 12 August 1947.

35 'The "Puck" Programme', *Kerry Champion*, 12 August 1933.

36 'Groping Back into the Mists of Antiquity', *Kerry Reporter*, 11 August 1934.

37 Liam Foley, 'Puck – The Mardi Gras of The South', *Kerryman*, 11 August 1945.

38 'The "Puck" Programme', *Kerry Champion*, 12 August 1933.

39 'Kerry's Great Harvest Fair and Carnival', *Kerryman*, 17 August 1935.

40 'At the Fair of Puck', *Kerry Reporter*, 18 August 1928.

41 Patrick Houlihan, *Cast a Laune Shadow: Reminiscences of Life in Killorglin* (1997) page 119.

42 'Former Lords of 99,000 Acres', *Irish Press*, 9 July 1936; 'Protecting Public Interest in Green', *Kerryman*, 24 December 1982.

43 Marie O'Reilly, 'I Sketch Your World', *Irish Independent*, 13 August 1948.

44 'Puck Fair'. Letter to the editor by Kieran Foley *et al. Irish Press*, 25 February 1967.

45 'Puck Fair. Kerry Town in Festive Garb', *Irish Press*, 12 August 1936.

46 'At the Fair of Puck', *Kerry Reporter*, 18 August 1928; 'Puck Fair', *Kerry Reporter*, 16 August 1930; Seán O'Faolain, *An Irish Journey* (Longmans, London, 1940) page 135.

47 'Puck Fair', *Kerryman*, 15 August 1931; 'Puck Fair. Kerry Town in Festive Garb', *Irish Press*, 12 August 1936.

48 Quoted in 'Life Goes to an Irish Party', *LIFE*, 29 September 1941, page 115.

49 'Killorglin Fair Boom', *Irish Independent*, 13 August 1940; 'Puck Fair Thronged', *Irish Press*, 11 August 1943.

50 'Puck Fair is Here Once More!', *Kerryman*, 7 August 1943; '1945 Puck Fair One of Best for Years', *Kerryman*, 18 August 1945.

51 Muriel Rukeyser, *The Orgy* (Andre Deutsch, London, 1965) pages 18 and 28.

52 Brian Barton, *Northern Ireland in the Second World War* (Ulster Historical Foundation, Belfast, 1995) page 11; Clair Wills, *That Neutral Ireland: A Cultural History of Ireland During the Second World War* (Faber and Faber, London, 2007) page 239.

53 'Thousands of Visitors at Puck Fair', *Irish Press*, 12 August 1947.

54 'Puck Fair', *Kerry Reporter*, 16 August 1930.

55 Frank Wilson, 'Fun and Sport in Kerry', *Kerry Reporter*, 11 August 1934.

56 E.E. O'Donnell (ed.), *Father Browne's Kerry* (Messenger Publications, Dublin, 2012) page 108.

57 Marie O'Reilly, 'I Sketch Your World', *Irish Independent*, 13 August 1948.

58 Frank Wilson, 'Fun and Sport in Kerry', *Kerry Reporter*, 11 August 1934.

59 Seán Crawford, 'Come to the Fair', *Irish Press*, 25 May 1939.

60 Michael Houlihan, *Puck Fair History and Traditions* (Treaty Press, Limerick, 1999) page 83.

61 'An Amazing Festival in County Kerry', *Meath Chronicle*, 26 July 1930.

62 Robert Gibbings, *Sweet Cork of Thee* (Dent, London, 1951), pages 206-207.

63 Stowers Johnson, *Before And After Puck* (Fortune Press, London, 1953) page 101.

64 'Kerry's Great Harvest Fair and Carnival', *Kerryman*, 17 August 1935; Richard Hayward, *In The Kingdom of Kerry* (Dundalgan Press, Dundalk, 1946) page 232.

65 'Puck Fair', by 'C'maine', *Kerry Reporter*, 11 August 1934.

66 'Kerry's Great Harvest Fair and Carnival', *Kerryman*, 17 August 1935.

67 Richard Hayward, *In The Kingdom of Kerry* (Dundalgan Press, Dundalk, 1946) page 232.

68 'Gypsies Fined for Obstruction', *Nenagh Guardian*, 26 March 1932.

69 'Police Battle with Gypsies', *Irish Press*, 15 February 1933.

70 'Gypsies Sentenced', *Irish Press*, 24 November 1939.

71 *Connacht Tribune*, 24 June 1944.

72 'Life Goes to an Irish Party', *LIFE*, 29 September 1941, page 117.

73 Stowers Johnson, *Before And After Puck* (Fortune Press, London, 1953) page 103.

74 Patrick Houlihan, *Cast a Laune Shadow: Reminiscences of Life in Killorglin* (1997) page 110.

75 'Puck Fair', *Kerry Reporter*, 16 August 1930; 'Kerry's Great Harvest Fair and Carnival', *Kerryman*, 17 August 1935.

76 Michael Houlihan, *Puck Fair History and Traditions* (Treaty Press, Limerick, 1999) page 106.

77 Una Lehane, 'William Bird: Patriarch of the Travelling Shows', *Irish Times*, 23 February 1980; 'Live Music in the Streets', *Kerryman*, 11 August 1989.

78 'Crowning the Luck', *Southern Star*, 2 November 1940; 'Puck Fair at Bantry', *Southern Star*, 27 September 1947; 'Parochial Carnival', *Southern Star*, 8 May 1948.

79 A.J.V. O'Reilly, 'Beneath Carrantuohill', *Irish Independent*, 15 July 1949.

80 Paddy Smyth, 'Puck Fair with a Difference – It Will Last For a Week', *Kerryman*, 7 August 1965.

81 'An Amazing Festival in County Kerry', *Meath Chronicle*, 26 July 1930.

82 'Puck Fair', *Kerry Reporter*, 16 August 1924.

83 *Ibid.*

84 'At the Fair of Puck', *Kerry Reporter*, 18 August 1928.

85 Local press advertisements for the Oisin Ballroom started appearing from March 1939.

86 The first advertisements for Lyons' Ballroom appeared in 1948; *Kerryman*, 15 May 1948.

87 Advertisement for Grand Opening of Laune Ballroom, *Kerryman*, 10 August 1940.

88 'Kerry's Great Harvest Fair and Carnival', *Kerryman*, 17 August 1935; advertisement for the Oisin Ballroom, *Kerryman*, 5 August 1939.

89 Advertisement for the Oisin Ballroom, *Kerryman*, 11 August 1945.

90 Stowers Johnson, *Before And After Puck* (Fortune Press, London, 1953) pages 93-94.

91 Garry Hogg, *Turf Beneath My Feet* (Museum Press, London, 1950) page 80.

92 Garry Hogg, *Turf Beneath My Feet* (Museum Press, London, 1950) page 72.

93 Roger McHugh, 'Did You Go To Puck?', in *Puck Fare*, Autumn, 1945 (Writers' Artists' Actors' and Musicians' Association, Dublin, 1945).

94 'The Festival of Puck', *Irish Independent*, 13 August 1938.

95 'An Amazing Festival in County Kerry', *Meath Chronicle*, 26 July 1930.

96 Stowers Johnson, *Before And After Puck* (Fortune Press, London, 1953) pages 122, 127, 128 and 129.

97 'The Festival of Puck', *Irish Independent*, 13 August 1938.

98 *Kerry Reporter*, 25 August 1928.

99 'An Amazing Festival in County Kerry', *Meath Chronicle*, 26 July 1930.

100 'Readers write of Mutton Pies', *Irish Independent*, 8 October 1959.

101 Mary Murphy, of Lower Bridge Street. See Michael Houlihan, *Puck Fair History and Traditions* (Treaty Press, Limerick, 1999) page 98.

102 Maurice O'Leary, 'Puck Will Be Crowned in Killorglin on Sunday', *Kerryman*, 11 August 1962.

103 Stowers Johnson, *Before And After Puck* (Fortune Press, London, 1953) page 81.

104 'An Amazing Festival in County Kerry', *Meath Chronicle*, 26 July 1930.

105 'All Eyes Will Be On Noreen', *Irish Times*, 12 August 1950.

106 'Life Goes to an Irish Party', *LIFE*, 29 September 1941, page 116.

107 Seán O'Faolain, *An Irish Journey* (Longmans, London, 1940) page 136.

108 'McGillicuddy's Killorglin'. Letter from Patrick McGillicuddy, *LIFE*, 20 October 1941, page 2.

109 'Irish-American Protest on Puck Fair Article', *Irish Press*, 27 November 1941.

110 Andrew Lycett, *Dylan Thomas: A New Life* (Phoenix, London, 2004) page 272.

111 Caitlin Thomas, *My Life With Dylan Thomas: Double Drink Story* (Virago, London, 2008) pages 96-98.

112 Patsy McGarry, 'Lost in the Mists of Puckology and Drink', *Irish Independent*, 12 August 1993, page 9.

113 Richard Hayward, *In the Kingdom of Kerry* (Dundalgan Presss, Dundalk, 1946) page 230.

114 Michael Houlihan, *Puck Fair History and Traditions* (Treaty Press, Limerick, 1999) pages 112 and 116.

115 These films can currently be seen at www.movietone.com.

116 'Enthroning King Puck', *Kerry Champion*, 8 August 1934; 'Puck Fair Quaint Kerry Ceremony on Saturday', *Anglo-Celt*, 11 August 1928; 'Puck Fair', *Kerryman*, 15 August 1931; 'Puck Fair Thronged', *Irish Press*, 11 August 1943.

117 'Puck Fair Quaint Kerry Ceremony on Saturday', *Anglo-Celt*, 11 August 1928.

118 'Puck Fair. Kerry Town in Festive Garb', *Irish Press*, 12 August 1936.

119 *Ibid.*

120 Richard Hayward, *In The Kingdom of Kerry* (Dundalgan Press, Dundalk, 1946) page 233.

121 'Puck Fair', *Kerry Reporter*, 16 August 1924; 'Puck Fair Opens', *Irish Press*, 13 August 1935; 'Puck Fair. Kerry Town in Festive Garb', *Irish Press*, 12 August 1936.

122 Richard Hayward, *In The Kingdom of Kerry* (Dundalgan Press, Dundalk, 1946) pages 234-236.

123 Robert Gibbings, *Sweet Cork of Thee* (Dent, London, 1951) pages 204-205.

124 'Puck Fair', *Kerryman*, 15 August 1931; 'Puck Fair Today', *Irish Press*, 12 August 1940.

125 'Killorglin', *Kerryman*, 18 August 1962; 'Oh, What a Puck!', *Kerryman*, 18 August 1962.

126 Richard Hayward, *In The Kingdom of Kerry* (Dundalgan Press, Dundalk, 1946) page 235.

127 Charles Duff, *Ireland and the Irish* (Boardman and Co., London, 1952) page 213.

128 'Thousands See "King Puck" Enthroned', *Irish Times*, 11 August 1955.

129 'At the Fair of Puck', *Kerry Reporter*, 18 August 1928 ('the coronation of the Puck'); 'Puck Fair', *Kerryman*, 15 August 1931 (The goat was 'duly elevated, enthroned and crowned').

130 *Puck Fair at Killorglin*. British Movietone News, 1935; Richard Hayward, *In The Kingdom of Kerry* (Dundalgan Press, Dundalk, 1946) page 235; '1945 Puck Fair One of Best for Years', *Kerryman*, 18 August 1945.

131 'All the Fun of Puck Fair', *Irish Independent*, 11 August 1937.

132 J.P. O'Sullivan, 'The Beauty of Puck Fair', *Kerry Champion*, 11 August 1951. *Gleann Scothaidhe*: Scotia's Glen. The queen's grave is supposed to lie under a large stone there.

133 Robert Gibbings, *Sweet Cork of Thee* (Dent, London, 1951) page 205.

134 Liam Foley, 'Puck – The Mardi Gras of the South', *Kerryman*, 11 August 1945.

135 'Thousands of Visitors at Puck Fair', *Irish Press*, 12 August 1947.

5

PUCK FAIR IN THE TOURIST AGE

By the middle of the 1950s some longstanding elements of Killorglin's commercial life had dwindled. In 1954, Liam Foley again noted decline.[1] The railway station, which had hosted eight trains a day, now had three. (The station closed for good in February 1960.) None of the several hotels which had operated in the previous decades continued to be run as hotels, and only one establishment, known as the Bridgeview (or Bridge) Hotel, was available from the late 1950s until the very early 1960s.[2] Although there were several new shops and petrol stations along the Iveragh Road, there were no local factories, and the increasing mechanisation of farming had reduced the work available for farm labourers. Killorglin, like the rest of Kerry and the nation as a whole, offered too few work opportunities, and emigration was rife. In 1911 the population of the greater Killorglin area was 4,053; by 1956 it was 2,938.[3] 'This town has died a slow death', a local man commented in 1959. 'Wages are low here and the chances for young people are few. They have no choice but to emigrate. For some, and indeed they are very few, Puck Fair makes all the difference between emigrating and being able to stay at home.'[4]

THE TOURISM SOLUTION

A partial solution to economic decline was to make Puck Fair ever more attractive to greater numbers of Irish sightseers and foreign tourists, who might be willing to spend more money in the town. This represented not so much a new policy, as the intensification of a continuing one. Accordingly, the organising committee expended a lot of effort during the 1950s and '60s in trying to find various diversions and amusements which they thought would be entertaining for visitors. In doing so, however, Puck Fair began a transformation, from a fair with carnival features attached, to a carnival with a fair attached.

Recognition of the need for changes followed two quieter fairs in 1953 and 1954. A local correspondent wrote after the latter:

> ... it is now agreed that the overall picture fell far short of that of last year, which in itself had shown a decline. A 25 per cent decline in receipts of the professional amusement centres but indicates a similar falling off in business in general

> An internationally known photographer[5] at the fair remarked upon the originality of so many people seeking and finding such innocent fun in a scene in which they were themselves the principal actors. The majority are fast demanding something more than the spectacle of a crowned goat to command their attention, and with the keen competition now offered by other centres for tourist trade, Killorglin people as a whole, and not merely a small committee, will have to throw their weight behind Puck Fair.[6]

Committee member Ted Mangan recalled in 1957 that 'some years back, it looked as if the Fair was on the way out'.[7]

New diversions began to be introduced to appeal to the public. At the fair of 1956 there was a Fancy Dress Parade, which followed the Laune Pipers as they escorted King Puck to the stand. There was a Soap-Box Derby, in which children raced in a variety of wheeled carts, made 'from golf caddy cars to outsize dolls prams'.[8] (The route went from the church, down hill to Bridge Street cross.)[9] An exhibition of mumming was presented; this was a regional style of dancing with batons, from County Wexford.[10] The biggest change, however, was that the dates of that year's fair were moved, so that the opening day was on a Sunday, and the fair took place on 12-14 August. This was to encourage a greater number of visitors who might want to attend the opening ceremonies without losing a working day.[11] The strategy seems to have paid off, as even though torrential rain fell throughout the day, there was reported to be a near record crowd.[12]

In 1957, a Donkey Derby was introduced.[13] The race started at the Puck Fair stand and ran along Upper Bridge Street, down Mill Road and along

New Line Road, and finished at the bridge.[14] The race proved to be highly popular among spectators and riders alike, and it became a feature of the fair for many years. Some difficulties subsequently arose, however:

> … the committee realising that the devious route followed in previous years gave rise to confusion, disregard of rules and unfair treatment of the animals participating, are making this year's race over a direct, short course which will at all times be under the observation of stewards and spectators – from the cottages at Dromavalla, across the bridge and up Main St.[15]

By 1962, heats for the donkey race 'drew large crowds during the fair and were a highlight of the programme though justifiably there was adverse criticism levelled at the treatment meted out by some of the itinerant class to their animals'.[16] Two years later, the event was cancelled over concerns about what a committee member termed 'the persistent cruelty of a few'.[17] But clearly the event was too popular to omit, and it was revived for the fair of 1965. It was nevertheless insisted that 'The Puck Fair Committee are leaving no stone unturned to ensure that no ill-treatment of the animals will take place. No sticks, stones or saddles will be allowed to be used and no

'Sold!', 1966. (© The Kennelly Archive)

104

rider will be permitted to strike his mount. In fact any rider found striking his mount "will be instantly" disqualified'.[18]

Further innovations were introduced in 1958. For the first time, a printed souvenir programme was produced, which examined some of the origin stories of the fair.[19] There was an Agricultural Parade and an Industrial Parade (the latter poorly subscribed).[20] A new role, that of 'hostess', was created, in which a woman dressed in 'traditional national costume' (a long, dark robe in vaguely 'Celtic' style) greeted visitors, and attended the girl-queen's crowning of the Puck goat.[21] (The role continued for a few years, but was phased out after 1962.)

Throughout the 1950s and '60s, there were many different attractions at the fair, including various sporting events, such as GAA challenge matches, drag-hunts, tug-of-war, and cycle races.[22] Several regattas were held, and at the fair of 1965 the boats taking part were the type used by local fishermen, known as 'bankers'; they were 18ft long and there were estimated to be about eighty of them in use in the greater Killorglin area.[23] Other events were of a traditional character; there was a ballad-singing contest (judged by folk-singer Liam Clancy), a Biddy competition, and a Wren Boy competition, the latter judged by Kerry playwright John B. Keane.[24] (Biddy contests consisted of men and boys dressed up as women and playing traditional instruments. Customarily, they visited local houses and performed music and dances for St Brigid's Day, 1 February, in exchange for food or money to allow them to host a party later on. The Biddy tradition was quite strong in the Killorglin area.[25] Wren Boys traditionally dressed in straw hats or costumes and paraded through towns and villages on 26 December, St Stephen's Day.)

The idea of disregarding the traditional dates for the fair persisted. In 1959 the event began with a carnival day on 9 Sunday, 'as an incentive to the holiday-maker',[26] and a plan was mooted to change the customary days for good and have every Puck Fair on the second Sunday of August.[27] In 1965, the event was held as a week-long 'Festival of Puck Fair', running from 8-15 August.[28]

In general, the attendance figures for the fair appear to have risen from the mid-1950s, although it must be remembered that the numbers cited, as always, seem to have been estimates by journalists or members of the committee. In 1958, 40,000 people visited, in 1960 there were 45,000, and in 1962 a record 60,000.[29] (Nevertheless, although there were reported to be 20,000 people at the Sunday pre-Puck carnival of 1959, there were said to be only 5,000 – 10,000 on the official Gathering Day following.)[30]

BUTTY SUGRUE, 'THE AMAZING BLONDINI', AND 'THE MONKEY MAN'

As well as the entertainments thought up by the Puck Fair committee, the fair itself regularly threw up its own amusements.

In 1953, Michael 'Butty' Sugrue (1924-1977), a former circus performer with Duffy's Circus and billed as 'Ireland's Strongest Man', staged a wrestling bout at the fair between himself and former boxer Jack Doyle. The contest took place after the goat coronation and was held in the open air at Langford Street.[31] Butty was from Gortnascarry, Killorglin, and liked to say that he had been brought up on a diet of 'raw meat and goat's milk'.[32] He was a squat, powerfully built man, who had developed his physique with the intention of becoming a professional wrestler. He became a strongman and a showman instead. During his career he pulled a double-decker bus through a Dublin street, and after moving to London he managed two pubs there, while occasionally demonstrating various feats of strength, such as clenching a chair between his teeth and lifting up a man or woman sitting on it.

Jack Doyle (1913-1978), nicknamed 'The Gorgeous Gael', was a friend of Sugrue from his connections in boxing circles. During the 1930s, the Cork man had at one time been a contender for the British Boxing Championship; before he had even become a professional fighter he had won twenty-eight successive victories, twenty-seven of those by knockout. But as his career went on he tended to suffer defeats as a result of doing his training in the pub beforehand, and retired. He was afterwards discovered to have a fine singing voice and he went on to record for the Decca label; he also had a small Hollywood acting career. By the 1950s, however, Doyle was a confirmed alcoholic, often reduced to living off the kindness of his friends, and Butty's wrestling match seems to have been conceived as a bit of an earner for them both. The bout was something of a non-event, with Doyle retiring after the first round due to injury.[33] Butty afterwards became a regular visitor to Puck Fair, and in 1966, dressed as a Celtic warrior, he pulled a cart carrying the goat up the street to the platform.[34]

Another ex-circus performer, 'The Amazing Blondini', appeared at Puck Fair in 1959. In reality he was Michael Costello (1922-1996). Although by his own account he had been born at a fairground in Dublin, to parents from Cork who were both circus performers, he was said, probably in an effort to drum-up local interest, to have been from nearby Cromane,[35] some five miles (eight kilometres) west of Killorglin.[36] From the age of thirteen he had struck out on his own, touring with various circuses in Ireland and Britain as a sword-swallower and fire-eater. After his young sister fell to her death in a trapeze accident he left the circus and began life as a drifter and sometime attraction in his own right. He was to perform twice a day at Puck Fair, engaging in a variety of daredevil activities:

> He is scheduled to blow himself up with dynamite in a coffin and pull buses through the town. If he survives these ordeals – and he must have exhausted the nine lives of a cat by now – he will throw himself from the Laune Bridge, tied in a mailbag. Blondini, will, of course, need a favouring tide under the bridge to perform this feat.[37]

During the 1950s, 'The Monkey Man' attended the fair. He was a Traveller from Limerick who ran a gambling game, and to attract punters he carried a small monkey about with him.[38] The animal clambered around his shoulders and crowds gathered to watch. The man would not reveal much about himself: 'I do not like my name in the papers', he once told a reporter.[39]

The Monkey Man, 1955. (© The Kennelly Archive)

STREET ENTERTAINMENT

Among the usual side-show games there was 'Kick-the-Ball',[40] in which punters had to kick a football attached to a stick and hit coloured balloons to win prizes;[41] this was one of the most popular games, and newspapers and magazines afterwards often pictured men and women having a go, legs stretched out in mid-kick.[42]

Traveller women told fortunes at different spots: at their caravans parked at the far side of the river, standing at the fair field, or, at night, under the coloured lights which were hung over the Laune bridge.[43] In 1957, a journalist with the *Kerryman* met fortune-teller Margaret Delaney, who said she had been coming to Puck Fair for twenty years. Unusually, she traded as 'Madam Lee', seemingly having adopted a common Romany gypsy name for effect.[44] Another reporter with the *Kerryman* watched at the fair of 1962:

> A young man with an eye to the 'future' was having his fortune told by fortune teller Bridget O'Brien, who, when asked where she came from, said 'no fixed abode, I suppose.' She was crossing her client's hand with silver – a half a crown with which he parted – and she told him of love and money and journeys across the sea.[45]
>
> Another visitor was told, ''Tis a fine young man like you should be on the look-out for a blonde with a black skirt on your first visit to Puck Fair – she will surely make you happy'.[46]

Riskier entertainment was offered by the 'Wheel of Fortune' stalls,[47] Three Card Trick players[48] and Trick o' the Loop men.[49] The Three Card Trick, also known as Find The Lady, was not a true gambling game at which a customer could win money, but a con trick operated through the dealer's sleight of hand. Three cards would be laid out, usually upon a cardboard box (which could be picked up quickly in the event of the arrival of the police). The money card that the mark was encouraged to bet upon finding was usually the Queen of Hearts, among two black cards, usually the Jack of Spades and Jack of Clubs. By holding and throwing down the cards in a certain way the dealer convinced the mark, incorrectly, that the money card could be identified, and a bet would be placed and lost. Occasionally, an accomplice was involved, to bet and to win or to encourage the mark to bet; he also kept a look out for the police. A photograph, which appears to date from the 1960s, of a Find the Lady operator and his nervous lookout man was reproduced by the *Kerryman* in 1987.[50] In 1956, four men from Limerick city, Charleville and Mallow, were fined for operating the trick,[51] and in 1966 another man from Limerick was charged with the same offence:

> Inspector R. Fahy said Gardai saw the defendant playing the three card trick. They saw him take £2-10 from a young man aged about 14. The injured party who was from Wexford was in Killorglin specially for Puck Fair. Justice J.B. O'Farrell gave the defendant 20 minutes to produce the money in court.[52]

Bird's Amusements appeared at the fair as usual. They had fairground rides such as chair-o-planes, dodgems, and hobby horses.[53] The famous fairground attraction, the 'Wall of Death', in which a motorcyclist drove up and around the inside of a steep circular wooden palisade, was presented in 1956.[54] Three years earlier, a giant 'Joy Wheel', 60ft high, which could give patrons a bird's-eye view of the event, had been introduced. The big wheel had over 100 coloured lights attached,[55] and during the 1950s, and for at least part of the '60s, the town and the Laune Bridge were also strung with coloured fairy lights,[56] so that Killorglin during the nights of the fair must have given a romantic impression to locals and tourists alike.

Happy revellers who wished to remember their experiences could buy souvenirs of Puck in Killorglin shops, such as Foley's Café on Iveragh Road;[57] plaster plaques of the goat were sold in Killorglin in the late 1950s.[58] Alternatively, visitors could get their photographs taken under a sign declaring them to be 'Loyal Subjects of His Majesty King Puck'.[59]

DANCING, DRINKING AND EATING

Night-time activities continued to include dancing. The Oisin Ballroom and Lyons' Ballroom were joined from July 1954 by the CYMS building in Mill Road, which featured a purpose-made sprung maple floor.[60] The ballrooms also served non-alcoholic drinks ('minerals') and ice creams.[61] The music was provided by outfits like Sam Locke and His Orchestra, and a number of small bands who played in the hugely popular 'showband' style (playing cover-versions of current popular music hits, while standing and performing some dance moves), such as The Royal Showband, The Clipper Carlton, and the Capitol Showband.[62]

During the 1950s and '60s there were thirty-two pubs in Killorglin[63] (although that number shrank a little as time went on, so that by 1969 there were twenty-six).[64] For them, Puck Fair was a financial bonanza, as they had traditionally stayed open continuously throughout, a fact which was well-known nationally. Canon Glynn of Galway, objecting to the extension of pub licensing hours for Galway Races in 1960, pleaded, 'What is wanted? A country fit for only boozers to live in? A country allowing drinking at all hours of the day and night? People should be in bed at midnight, races or no races. Galway is not like Puck Fair.'[65] In a Dáil debate about pub licensing in 1962, Mayo TD Henry Kenny complained that pubs serving the pilgrims to Croagh Park should get special concessions: 'This was a traditional pilgrimage. Puck Fair had got such a concession and it was a pagan festival'.[66]

Although the pubs of Killorglin received generous exemption orders through applications to the courts, they were still supposed to close for one hour, between 1 a.m. and 2 a.m. in the morning. For years that rule was not enforced,[67] and, in addition, publicans sometimes served drinkers after hours on the night before Puck Fair even began; fining two publicans and the customers found on the premises on 9 August 1953, the judge insisted that 'these pre-Puck festivities must not again be confused with Puck Fair proper'.[68]

Consternation reigned among the pub owners of Killorglin, when, in 1960, the letter of the law began to be insisted upon in relation to closing for an hour.

Enforcement of the order means that the age-old tradition of keeping all doors open for the three days and nights of Puck must be broken.

One resident told our Reporter: 'The granting of the exemption order to Puck is something which is very old and was never abused.'

The publicans are anxious to obey the Law as outlined by the Gardai but are in a quandary as how to do so. 'What can we do?' asked one publican. 'The town will have up to 50,000 people each night and how can we clear our premises?'[69]

After that year's fair the publicans of Killorglin said that they had lost £100 each by having to close for the hour.[70]

During the day there was plenty to eat at Puck Fair. About forty restaurants and informal eateries operated for the duration.[71] During the 1950s and '60s at least one establishment was serving hot dogs, possibly for the American visitors.[72] Traditional fare included gingerbread, dillisk seaweed, and periwinkles, all eaten as snacks.[73] Salmon, poached from the Laune River, was sold on the street or supplied to restaurants:[74] in 1956, a fishery inspector and his men had to patrol the riverbank to prevent fish from being taken during the event.[75]

Of course, there were also 'good steaming Crubeens': in the early 1950s, Tralee butcher Frank Mulcahy travelled to the fair where he shouted out his wares;[76] in 1959 local butcher Patrick O'Regan was selling 4 tons worth of these pigs' feet to local restaurants.[77] These were eaten with relish; in 1960, a *Kerryman* reporter met a happy fair-goer, 'with the grease of a crubeen dripping from his bristling foxy moustache and the odour of Guinness on his breath'.[78] It was estimated that 10 tons of crubeens and 20 tons of beef, mutton and ham were consumed during the fair.[79]

Television Cameras Arrive

The spectacle of a goat crowned as a king and all the attendant activities of the fair made for perfect visual material for the new medium of television.[80] As early as 1952 a broadcast from the fair was discussed between the Puck Fair committee and an unnamed British TV company. A year later, the BBC and the National Broadcasting Association of America filmed the crowning ceremony,[81] and the BBC returned in 1958.[82]

During the 1960s, interest from TV companies grew further, and there were two crews from the UK and France at the fair of 1962,[83] and three crews the following year.[84] The latter included the Canadian Broadcasting Corporation, who were making a film about Ireland.[85] 'It started off well enough', wrote three young Irishwomen, who viewed the TV broadcast of the film afterwards in Toronto:

> Then we moved to Killorglin for the Puck Fair celebrations, where the cameras lingered long and lovingly for the next 15 minutes or so in the atmosphere of a public house where we were given a rendering of some

Irish airs by a quartet of no particular singing ability and where one of the young men looked as if he hadn't combed his hair since the night before.

Then we had an ample viewing of stout being poured from a barrel and counters being wiped. Next the cameras roved over various customers and we were given time in which to see a man flat against the wall in an advanced state of drunkenness and the voice of another drunk interrupting the general noise and a fiddle being played by a tinker man. The cameras then flashed back to more beer being poured and more mopping of counters. Later, we were taken for a stroll through the streets where we were shown some weather beaten and unkempt looking spectators looking open-mouthed at the Irish dancing ... the attraction there seemingly was to concentrate on the inane expressions of the spectators.

More tinkers were shown and two women about to start a fight and in case we had missed it the first time the cameras returned a couple of times to the terrifying scene.[86]

'Is this how Ireland should be depicted to the world in 1964?' the letter writers complained.

In 1964, five companies filmed at the fair,[87] and in the following year there were crews from Irish television, as well as crews from Britain, America, Germany, Spain and New Zealand.[88] In these two years the crowning ceremony was staged twice, for the benefit of the TV cameras.[89]

THE TRAVELLERS ARE NO LONGER WANTED

During the period when Puck Fair was becoming an object of attention from the TV cameras, courting increasing numbers of tourists, the Travellers began to be viewed in a more negative light than previously.

There were two particular complaints against them, the first being the practice of begging. During the fair, children often roamed the streets pleading for coppers.[90] Women carrying children called into pubs looking for money from customers, and in 1958 Muriel Rukeyser saw a publican kick a begging Traveller woman hard to the ground.[91] Street begging was not only carried out by some Traveller women during the fair itself, but was also done in the two-week period following their arrival in the

Killorglin area before Puck Fair began. The local correspondent of the *Kerryman* complained:

'Spare a copper, and help a poor woman.' This plaintive appeal oft uttered down the ages, has gathered momentum in recent weeks. Every summer, and particularly during the weeks preceding Puck Fair, visitors have found good reason to complain, but this year they are being pestered right, left and centre. The 'travelling class' seem to make this part of the country their happy hunting-ground. They stay put in the environs by night and roam the streets by day. We have a duty to ourselves and to the fair name of our country to discharge, and something should be done about it. Our visitors must be sent away with kind thoughts and memories.[92]

Anne Lucey, who lived about ten miles from the town, remembered Travellers calling in the late 1960s:

They would come first in dribs and drabs, the same ones calling to the door as usual. The good travellers always came early. The world was easily divided into good and bad when we were children. Though quite what distinctions these huge things rested upon, I have yet to discover. We had our own notions.

The old traveller woman my mother liked was certainly good. She would come for the grain of tea and the bit of sugar and the 'sup' of milk and accept it with a 'God bless you, ma'm'.[93]

The second complaint about the Travellers concerned the state of their encampment after departure, where rubbish was left strewn about.[94] These issues were not new, but now Killorglin lay under the gazes of the tourists and the television cameras.

In 1955, the Travellers had been invited to take part in a competitive parade, showing off their traditional horse-drawn wooden caravans on the last day of the fair.[95] A total of ninety-five caravans took part.[96] (The best was judged to be that of a Mr Doherty, from Ballyshannon, County Donegal.)[97] By 1958, however, the Travellers were less welcome. In that year, stallholders, who were usually Travellers, were prohibited by the committee from pitching their stalls around the base of the Puck stand.[98] For the following year's fair,

Kerry County Council proposed that their caravans no longer be allowed to come within some distance of the town[99] (probably not within a three-mile radius, which was the distance insisted upon in 1960).[100] An earlier attempt to keep the caravans out of the Baile Nua housing estate, which lay beside their traditional riverside encampment, had ended up with the barrier being flung into the river.[101]

Not all the local people were happy with this change. A journalist with the *Kerryman* reported that:

> While some of the residents were hesitant to claim that the travelling class were an asset to the Gathering, others believed that without the tinkers much of the glamour of the fair would be lost.
>
> Another leading citizen told me that he did not agree with the clearing of the stalls and thimble riggers from around the Stand of the Puck Goat. 'We want them all as they all add up to Puck.' He believed that if the present trend was allowed to continue it would eventually result in having to send invitations to the travelling people to attend the fair.[102]

Quarantining the Travellers' encampments three miles away from Killorglin was tantamount to banning them from the fair altogether. However, at the fair of 1960, the Travellers initially parked about a quarter of a mile outside the town.[103] Gardai went down to enforce the County Council bye-law, notices of which had been put up along the Killarney road, and discovered a man from Donegal sitting in his caravan, for whom they held a three-year-old arrest warrant in respect of an incident at a previous Puck Fair. They collared him and brought him to Limerick jail, and in their absence, the others made a concerted rush forward, with both their traditional caravans and motorised vans and re-took their old standings at the far side of the Laune bridge. Over fifty caravans remained parked at their usual spot for the remainder of the fair. One man commented, 'We were getting no enjoyment out of the Fair being parked so far out, so we decided to move to our old camping ground.' He added, 'Sure, it's the travellers that make the fair'.[104] In response, the organisers quickly broadcast over the loudspeakers for the Court Clerk to attend the Garda station so that summonses to appear in court could be issued to the Travellers before they scattered after the fair.[105] The issue seems to have been resolved through the provision of a field for caravan parking, for which there was a daily charge, although it flared up occasionally again in years when no field was provided.[106]

Further restrictions followed for the next year's fair, when street traders were required to make contact with the committee beforehand, to be issued with 'authorisation cards', which would be granted at the discretion of the organisers, and without which their stalls could be prohibited.[107] In 1962, Traveller men and women were refused entry into one of the town's dance halls. Afterwards, they went on to express their frustration by gathering 100-strong and throwing bottles at a Garda on duty at the bridge, so that a force of his colleagues was required to drive the crowd out of the town. (Naturally, such scenes recalled the Traveller fights of the nineteenth century, and one local resident enthused, 'We have not witnessed a scene like this for years. It was like old times.')[108]

While the number of Travellers who attended Puck Fair varied from year to year, the official change of attitude towards them appears to have occurred at a period when their numbers were, in fact, dropping. It was said of the fair of 1954 that 'It was noticeable this year that many of these families were missing, and those that came said that it might be their last visit'.[109] It was said again in 1957, that 'A noticeable feature of this year's Fair was the small number of travelling people, in comparison with that of other years. I only counted 20 caravans parked on the Killarney Road'.[110]

Part of the reason for the fewer numbers may have been that Puck's horse fairs, the Travellers' traditional draw, were not what they were. In Killorglin, five harness-makers had once plied their trade, but by 1955 there was only one left, which was indicative of the falling off in the use of farm workhorses locally.[111] Tractors continued to replace horses and one of the few groups looking for working animals at Puck Fair were the pony-men from the Gap of Dunloe and the jarveys of Killarney, who carried tourists to various sights.[112]

There were fewer opportunities for Traveller men to engage in 'horse blocking' or 'horse tangling', a process by which a Traveller inserted himself into the bargaining and argument being engaged in by the buyer and the seller of a horse, and brought about a resolution and a sale. The Travellers' traditional knowledge of horses, which was acknowledged by the settled community, meant that they could talk up the merits of the animal. When the two parties concluded the sale, the seller usually paid the blocker a small amount, and by carrying on through the horse fair for the day, money could be earned.

By 1964, according to Michael Houlihan, then retired as the long-time goat-catcher of the fair, there had been an 'almost total disappearance' of Travellers compared to earlier years.[113] In the previous year, they were reported hardly to have appeared at all.[114]

If horse dealing and horse blocking faded as a source of income for the Travellers, there were still other means by which to make some money. Away from Puck Fair they went into the scrap-metal business; while at the fair, there were still opportunities for stallholders, ballad singers and musicians. Women also read palms or did some begging. Several Traveller children were musicians: at the fair of 1958, youngsters Patrick, John and Jeremiah Dunne were photographed with banjo, accordion and fiddle; 'They are natives of Tralee, they explained, but travel around in a caravan'.[115]

There was a particular boost in August 1961, when a film company went to Inch beach to shoot scenes for a version of J.M. Synge's *The Playboy of the Western World*, starring feted Irish actress Siobhán McKenna, and Travellers were recruited as extras. There, five families got six week's work:

> For the first time in 20 years horse dealer Johnny 'boy' Quilligan was not at the fair with his covered caravan, wife and family of four. 'Who would be at Puck when I can get £5 a day from the film company for the hire of myself, the wagon and horse and the family. Into the bargain I get £1 a day for fodder for my horses.'[116]

CHANGES TO THE LIVESTOCK FAIR

Like other aspects of Puck Fair during the 1950s and '60s, the most traditional element of it, the livestock fair, also underwent changes. The most important of these was that Gerald Foley, the Baron of the Fair, sold to the Irish Land Commission his family's right to collect tolls due on every animal sold.[117] Previously, the roads exiting Killorglin would have been blocked by wooden trestles set up by his men, dressed in long drover's coats, demanding payment and carrying stout sticks.[118] But at the fair of 1957, Gerald declared, 'Killorglin is now a free port!'[119] A right which the Foley family appear to have exercised since about the year 1800, had passed forever.

While the horse fair had declined, the sales of pigs and cattle remained good. At the fair of 1956 over 750 pigs were offered for sale and there were pig buyers from Tralee, Cork, Limerick, and the North-West of Ireland.[120] As for cattle, 5,000 of them, including many of the local Kerry breed, were driven to Killorglin for the fair of 1959.[121]

After the railway station closed in 1960, state transport company CIE constructed cattle pens at the railway yard, capable of carrying between 300 and 400 animals, and from there it moved the cattle in trucks to Killarney station for onward transport by rail.[122]

Before the fair of 1963, rumours were spread that typhoid fever had hit the town. An incident at the end of June, when two children had become sick, but recovered, 'was magnified into the threat of a full scale typhoid epidemic and visitors were advised by outside sources not to come to Puck, not to stay long, or to bring with them their own food and drink. The committee are unanimous that if the originators of the scare headlines could be identified they would take the necessary legal action against them'.[123] Many of the cattle and horse dealers avoided entering Killorglin and instead conducted their business on the outskirts of the town; this had a knock-on affect on the cafés and restaurants, who suffered a significant loss of business.[124]

THE GOAT CEREMONY

The goat ceremony underwent some changes, but these were mostly slight. As mentioned, there was a new adult role of hostess, accompanying that of the girl-queen, but this does not seem to have lasted more than a handful of years. While the queen continued to crown the goat, the de-crowning at the end of the fair appears to have been done by a young pageboy.[125]

There are conflicting reports about the use of torchlight processions during some of the dethronement ceremonies of the 1950s. The ceremony of 1953 was supposed to have included a torchlight procession,[126] but another account suggests it did not actually take place.[127] The same fiery attraction was scheduled for the end of the fair of 1957, but again no confirmation exists to affirm that it went ahead.[128]

In fact, the dethronement ceremonies may have declined as spectacles from the late 1950s onwards. Muriel Rukeyser viewed the dethronement of 1958, which she described as unattended, and she watched afterwards as the goat was put into a van, the crown thrown in after him, and he was driven away.[129] The press and TV attention which focused on the hoisting ceremony may have boosted that element at the expense of the lowering ceremony; from the 1960s up until present day, the dethronement appears to have been reduced to a minor event, in marked contrast to the ceremonies of the nineteenth and early twentieth Centuries, when the lowering of the goat had been very much a celebrated event in itself.

SEÁN O'SHEA

Michael Houlihan retired in 1955, and his son, Patrick, oversaw the supply of the goat to the stand.[130] From about 1953 the goat was provided by farmer Seán O'Shea (d.1971), of Glencuttane, Glencar, in the MacGillycuddy Reeks mountains.[131] On the occasion of his own retirement, in 1985, Pa Houlihan explained the procedure to a journalist, who summarised, 'Every year Seán O'Shea used to round up a herd of goats on the Macgillycuddy's Reeks and have them in an accessible place for the Houlihans'. One of the men would then go up to the farm and 'pick up a goat from where he had left him cor[r]alled and ready to bring to Killorglin'.[132] Not only was the goat supplied from farm stock, but the same animal was sometimes used again; such as happened from 1957 until 1960.[133]

PUCK FAIR NOT A TOURIST ATTRACTION

After all their efforts to increase the variety of attractions, to court tourists and host television crews, it must have been galling for the organisers when Bord Fáilte, the Irish tourist board, told them that Puck Fair was not a tourist event, and consequently would not be given financial assistance.

Before the fair of 1959, the fair's committee secretary, James Coffey, felt that Bord Fáilte should provide a grant to the Puck Fair committee 'for what is one of the biggest tourist attractions in the country'.[134] At a meeting held afterwards, the committee agreed to approach the tourist board formally.[135] By June the following year, they had had no reply,[136] and it was not until shortly before the fair of that year that they were informed by the tourism body that, in their view, Puck Fair was not a tourist attraction.[137] By 1961, the committee was finding that there were insufficient funds to run the event and two years later they again approached Bord Fáilte, but no progress was made.[138]

The tourist board instead went on to fund and support the Rose of Tralee festival, held at the end of August. The Tralee event hosted young women on stage who represented Irish communities at home and across the world, and who competed to be the winning Rose. It was clean, wholesome entertainment, designed to appeal to the propriety of the newly affluent urban middle classes of the 1960s. It could not have formed more of a contrast to Puck Fair, with its shouting stallholders, pubs full of raucous drinkers and streets full of farm animals. 'This was not the Ireland to which Bord Fáilte wanted to direct tourists', later commented Eric Zuelow in his analysis of how the fair was viewed by official Ireland during this time.[139]

INSUFFICIENT FUNDS AND NOT ENOUGH VOLUNTEERS

Without official help, the Puck Fair committee had to continually source funds from among the townspeople for the ever-increasing range of entertainments designed to attract tourists to what was said not to be a tourist attraction. By 1964, some additional money was coming from sponsorship by the drinks company, Guinness, without which, said chairman Declan Mangan, 'Puck Fair could not survive'.[140]

Another problem was the difficulty of getting people to help the committee. In May 1959 a spokesman explained that too few volunteers were turning up to planning meetings; 'The officers interpret this attitude as meaning that the townspeople do not care if Puck Fair is held in August. Three or four people cannot shoulder the burden of putting on the event. The officers appeal to all local clubs and organisations for assistance. If they do not get it the fair will have to be abandoned'.[141]

Five years later, a committee member once again expressed his disappointment:

They have in Puck Fair the only worthwhile industry in town. Killorglin depends on Puck Fair for its living but the business people do not realise this. They have shown a complete lack of interest in the whole affair and when the big event is over they just criticise the effort put into it by the officers and the few loyal committee members who week after week gave up valuable time to attend meetings and look after the affairs of Puck Fair.[142]

Among those who gave least of themselves, were those who benefited the most – the local publicans; 'These very men have, on the whole, been conspicuous by their absence from the organising committee over the past few years – despite appeals to them for support', wrote members of the committee.[143]

The twin refrains of insufficient funds and the deficiency in local involvement in organising Puck Fair were repeated regularly throughout the 1960s, yet the event continued to be presented successfully to the public, who were unaware of the issues that threatened to overwhelm it.

It was not until the 1970s, however, that it began to look like Puck Fair might no longer take place.

Notes

1 Liam Foley, 'Killorglin', *Kerryman*, 11 December 1954.
2 Advertisement, *Kerryman*, 23 March 1957; advertisement, *Kerryman*,
   2 December 1961. This business may have been the former Taylor's Hotel.
3 'Killorglin, internationally famous home of Puck Fair, is a dying town', *Kerryman*,
   31 October 1959.
4 *Ibid.*
5 Inge Morath (1923-2002), the celebrated photographer who worked for the
   Magnum Photos agency.
6 'Killorglin', *Kerryman*, 21 August 1954.
7 'Killorglin had 50,000 Visitors', *Kerryman*, 17 August 1957.
8 Brendan Malin, 'No Credit-Squeeze on the Puck Fair!', *Kerryman*, 11 August 1956.
9 'Caravans of the Travelling People Taking Up their Positions', *Kerryman*,
   9 August 1958.
10 Brendan Malin, 'Storm in Killorglin, but Nothing can Dampen Puck', *Kerryman*,
   18 August 1956.
11 'Warming up for the Festivities', *Kerryman*, 11 August 1956.
12 'Storm in Killorglin, but Nothing can Dampen Puck', *Kerryman*, 18 August 1956.
13 'Puck Fair is the Magnet and it Opens on Sunday', *Kerryman*, 10 August 1957.
14 'Caravans of the Travelling People Taking Up their Positions', *Kerryman*, 9 August 1958.
15 'Puck Fair Goes On – Without Aid', *Kerryman*, 15 July 1961.
16 'Killorglin', *Kerryman*, 18 August 1962.

17 '20,000' at Puck Fair, *Irish Press*, 10 August 1964.

18 Paddy Smyth, 'Puck Fair with a Difference – It Will Last for a Week', *Kerryman*, 7 August 1965.

19 Written by Michael P. Morris. Reproduced as 'Puck Fair – Killorglin Ireland's Oldest Fair and Carnival' in Paddy MacMonagle, *Paddy Mac's Shreds & Patches* (Mac Publications, Killarney, 2010).

20 Brendan Malin, 'The Goat Must Carry Puck on his Ample Back', *Kerryman*, 16 August 1958.

21 'Caravans of the Travelling People Taking Up their Positions', *Kerryman*, 9 August 1958; photographs of the hostess of 1958 can be viewed at the website of The Kennelly Archive, www.kennellyarchive.com.

22 'Puck Fair Carnival', *Kerryman*, 11 July 1959; 'Puck Fair Plans are Finalised', *Kerryman*, 17 July 1965; 'New Items on Puck Fair Programme This Year', *Kerryman*, 16 March 1963; 'Carnival Time Begins on Sunday', *Kerryman*, 5 August 1967.

23 Paddy Smyth, 'Puck Fair with a Difference – It Will Last for a Week', *Kerryman*, 7 August 1965.

24 Ian O'Leary, 'Publicans will see Puck Fair Coronation for the first time', *Kerryman*, 8 August 1964; 'Carnival Time Begins on Sunday', *Kerryman*, Aug 5, 1967; Paddy Smyth, 'Puck Fair with a Difference – It Will Last for a Week', *Kerryman*, 7 August 1965.

25 Paddy Smyth, 'Puck Fair with a Difference – It Will Last for a Week', *Kerryman*, 7 August 1965.

26 'Puck Fair', *Kerryman*, 9 May 1959.

27 Paddy Smyth, 'Puck Programme to be changed in 1960?', *Kerryman*, 15 August 1959.

28 Paddy Smyth, 'Puck Fair with a Difference – It Will Last for a Week', *Kerryman*, 7 August 1965.

29 'Mystery Was How So Many Got Into Killorglin', *Kerryman*, 16 August 1958; 'Puck Fair Plans Almost Complete', *Kerryman*, 22 July 1961; '60,000 see "Puck" crowned', *Irish Press*, 13 August 1962.

30 P.W. Smyth, 'Sunday's Hosting the Biggest Ever', *Kerryman*, 15 August 1959.

31 Patrick Houlihan, *Cast a Laune Shadow: Reminiscences of Life in Killorglin* (1997) pages 121-122.

32 Seamus Counihan, 'Butty's Biggest Gamble', *Sunday Independent*, 9 July 1972.

33 'Big Hosting at Puck Fair', *Nenagh Guardian*, 15 August 1953.

34 Michael Houlihan, *Puck Fair History and Traditions* (Treaty Press, Limerick, 1999) page 93.

35 'London Pipers Will Usher in Great Festival on Monday', *Kerryman*, 8 August 1959.

36 Gordon Thomas, *Bed of Nails: The Story of the Amazing Blondini* (Wingate, London, 1955) page 12.

37 'London Pipers Will Usher in Great Festival on Monday', *Kerryman*, 8 August 1959.

38 P.W. Smyth, 'Sunday's Hosting the Biggest Ever', *Kerryman*, 15 August 1959.

39 'Killorglin Had 50,000 Visitors', *Kerryman*, 17 August 1957. A photograph of the Monkey Man can be seen in Michael Houlihan's *Puck Fair History and Traditions* (Treaty Press, Limerick, 1999) page 59.

40 Paddy Smyth, 'Puck Fair with a Difference – It Will Last for a Week', *Kerryman*, 7 August 1965.

41 'Killorglin Had 50,000 Visitors', *Kerryman*, 17 August 1957.

42 'Killorglin Had 50,000 Visitors', *Kerryman, 17 August 1957;* 'Flashback. Puck of the Irish', *National Geographic Magazine*, Vol. 209, Issue 3, March 2006.

43 'Killorglin had 50,000 Visitors', *Kerryman*, 17 August 1957; 'Home of Puck Fair' *Kerryman*, 11 August 1956.

44 'Killorglin had 50,000 Visitors', *Kerryman*, 17 August 1957.

45 'Oh, What a Puck!' *Kerryman*, 18 August 1962.

46 *Ibid.*

47 Muriel Rukeyser, *The Orgy* (Andre Deutsch, London, 1965) page 160.

48 'Killorglin Prepares for the Three Days of Puck', *Kerryman*, 11 August 1956.

49 Ian O'Leary, 'Publicans will see Puck Fair Coronation for the First Time', *Kerryman*, 8 August 1964.

50 'Find The Lady!', captioned photograph, *Kerryman*, 7 August 1987.

51 'Four Men Fined at Killorglin', *Kerryman*, 22 December 1956.

52 'Three Card Trick Man gets Benefit of Probation Act', *Kerryman*, 13 August 1966.

53 P.W. Smyth, 'Puck Programme to be Changed in 1960?', *Kerryman*, 15 August 1959.

54 'Killorglin Prepares for the Three Days of Puck', *Kerryman*, 11 August 1956.

55 'Puck – The Fair that is Different the Festival that is Unique', *Kerryman*, 8 August 1953.

56 'Bad Weather Made Little Difference to Puck Fair', *Kerryman*, 18 August 1956; 'Puck Fair Plans Almost Complete', *Kerryman*, 22 July 1961; 'Lighting Bridge for Puck Fair', *Kerryman*, 16 May 1964.

57 Advertisement for Foley's Café, *Kerryman*, 9 August 1952.

58 Muriel Rukeyser, *The Orgy* (Andre Deutsch, London, 1965) page 109.

59 Photographs from The Kennelly Archive, www.kennellyarchive.com.

60 'Killorglin Prepares for the Three Days of Puck', *Kerryman*, 11 August 1956; advertisement for 'CYMS Maple Ballroom Killorglin', *Kerryman*, 11 August 1956; advertisement for Grand opening Night, *Kerryman*, 24 July 1954.

61 Advertisement for 'CYMS Maple Ballroom Killorglin', *Kerryman*, 11 August 1956.

62 'London Pipers Will Usher In Great Festival On Monday', *Kerryman*, 8 August 1959; 'Publicans will see Puck Fair Coronation for the First Time', *Kerryman*, 8 August 1964.

63 'King Puck's Subjects Sleep Four in a Bed', *Irish Times*, 10 August 1955; 'Three-Day Puck Fair Begins', *Irish Independent*, 11 August 1960.

64 'Business and Pleasure are Mixed at Puck Fair', *Kerryman*, 9 August 1969.

65 ''Savagery' Indictment by priest in Galway Race Week Application', *Sunday Independent*, 24 July 1960.

66 'Drinking hours on Sunday Discussed', *Irish Press*, 28 June 1962.

67 'Puck: Shock of a Closed Hour', *Irish Press*, 11 August 1960.

68 'Pre-Coronation Festivities in Killorglin', *Kerryman*, 17 October 1953.

69 Maurice F. O'Leary, 'Puck Fair in Full Blast', *Kerryman*, 13 August 1960.

70 'Puck Fair Closes', *Irish Independent*, Aug 13, 1960.

71 P.W. Smyth, 'Puck Fair is an Event Unique Throughout World', *Kerryman*, 8 August 1959.

72 Muriel Rukeyser, *The Orgy* (Andre Deutsch, London, 1965) page 144; Maurice O'Leary, 'Oh, What A Puck!', *Kerryman*, 18 August 1962.

73 Maurice F. O'Leary, 'Puck Fair in Full Blast', *Kerryman*, 13 August 1960; Muriel Rukeyser, *The Orgy* (Andre Deutsch, London, 1965) page 109.

74 Jim Edwards, 'A 'fine' fair for poachers', *Irish Times*, 16 May 1956.

75 'Bad Weather Made Little Difference to Puck Fair', *Kerryman*, 18 August 1956.

76 'Bad Weather Made Little Difference to Puck Fair', *Kerryman*, Aug 18, 1956.

77 P.W. Smyth, 'Puck Fair is an Event Unique Throughout World', *Kerryman*, 8 August 1959.

78 Maurice F O'Leary, 'Puck Fair in Full Blast', *Kerryman*, 13 August 1960.

79 Maurice O'Leary, 'Puck Will Be Crowned in Killorglin on Sunday', *Kerryman*, 11 August 1962.

80 For more on the television, cinema and newsreel attention directed to the fair over the years see Seán Moraghan, 'Puck Fair in Cinema and Television', *The Kerry Magazine*, Issue 23, 2013, pages 30-31.

81 'Big Hosting at Puck Fair', *Nenagh Guardian*, 15 August 1953.

82 'Caravans of the Travelling People Taking Up their Positions', *Kerryman*, 9 August, 1958.

83 '60,000 see "Puck" Crowned', *Irish Press*, 13 August 1962.

84 'Puck Fair Committee Asks For Greater Support', *Kerryman*, 26 January 1963.

85 *Horseman, Pass By*, Canadian Broadcasting Corporation, 1964.

86 'Our Image in Canada'. Letter by 'Three Optimists', Toronto. *Irish Press*, 6 April 1964.

87 '20,000 at Puck Fair', *Irish Press*, 10 August 1964.

88 'A Double Crowning for His Majesty!', *Kerryman*, 14 August 1965.

89 Ian O'Leary, 'Publicans will see Puck Fair Coronation for the First Time', *Kerryman*, 8 August 1964; 'A Double Crowning for His Majesty!', *Kerryman*, 14 August 1965.

90 Muriel Rukeyser, *The Orgy* (Andre Deutsch, London, 1965) page 110.

91 *Ibid.*

92 'Killorglin', *Kerryman*, 25 July 1953.

93 Anne Lucey, 'Timeless Puck Measures a Changing Life', *Kerryman*, 6 August 1993.

94 'Killorglin', *Kerryman*, 18 August 1962.

95 Liam Foley, 'Parade of Tinker Caravans on Last Day of Puck', *Kerryman*, 6 August 1955.

96 'King Puck's Subjects Sleep Four in a Bed', *Irish Times*, 10 August 1955.

97 'This Year's Puck in Perspective', *Kerryman*, 20 August 1955.

98 'Caravans of the Travelling People Taking Up their Positions', *Kerryman*, 9 August 1958.

99 'The Tinker Nuisance at Puck Fair', *Kerryman*, 6 September 1958.

100 Eileen Coughlan, 'In Killorglin', *Irish Press*, 7 April 1960.

101 'Killorglin', *Kerryman*, 31 July 1954.

102 'Caravans of the Travelling People Taking Up their Positions', *Kerryman*, 9 August 1958.

103 'Puck: Shock of a Closed Hour', *Irish Press*, 11 August 1960.

104 Maurice F. O'Leary, 'Puck Fair in Full Blast', *Kerryman*, 13 August 1960.

105 *Ibid.*

106 'Playboy Kept Them from Fair', *Irish Press*, 11 August 1961.

107 'Puck Fair Goes On – Without Aid', *Kerryman*, 15 July 1961; 'Puck Fair Plans Finalised', *Kerryman*, 5 August 1961.

108 'Peace of Puck Disturbed', *Kerryman*, 18 August 1962.

109 'Killorglin', *Kerryman*, 21 August 1954.

110 'Killorglin had 50,000 Visitors', *Kerryman*, 17 August 1957.

111 'Thought of My Coronation Makes Me Feel Just Like a Kid Again', *Kerryman*, 6 August 1960.

112 Maurice F. O'Leary, 'The Lure and Colour of Puck Lives On!', *Kerryman*, 15 August 1959.

113 Paddy Smith, 'He Has Put Many Kings on their Thrones', *Kerryman*, 8 August 1964.

114 'Killorglin Puck Fair Attracts Huge Crowds', *Irish Times*, 12 August 1963.

115 Brendan Malin, 'The Goat Must Carry Puck on his Ample Back', *Kerryman*, 16 August 1958.

116 'Playboy Kept Them from Fair', *Irish Press*, 11 August 1961.

117 Maurice F O'Leary, 'Puck Fair in Full Blast', *Kerryman*, 13 August 1960.

118 'Killorglin', in *Kerry County Guide and Maps* (Irish and Overseas Publishing Co., *c.* 1964) page 65.

119 'Killorglin had 50,000 Visitors', *Kerryman*, 17 August 1957.

120 Brendan Malin, 'Storm in Killorglin, but Nothing can Dampen Puck', *Kerryman*, 18 August 1956.

121 'At the Opening of Puck Fair', *Irish Independent*, 12 August 1959.

122 'Puck Fair Filming Finalised', *Kerryman*, 2 July 1960; Maurice O'Leary, 'Puck Will Be Crowned in Killorglin on Sunday', *Kerryman*, 11 August 1962.

123 'Killorglin Satisfied but Angry after Puck', *Kerryman*, 24 August 1963.

124 'Quiet Close to Puck Fair', *Irish Times*, 14 August 1963.

125 'Killorglin Crowded For End of Puck Fair', *Irish Independent*, 15 August 1956.

126 'Big Hosting at Puck Fair', *Nenagh Guardian*, 15 August 1953.

127 'Puck – The Fair that is Different the Festival that is Unique', *Kerryman*, 8 August 1953.

128 'Puck Fair is the Magnet and it Opens on Sunday', *Kerryman*, 10 August 1957.

129 Muriel Rukeyser, *The Orgy* (Andre Deutsch, London, 1965) page 175.

130 Michael Houlihan, *Puck Fair History and Traditions* (Treaty Press, Limerick, 1999); Brendan Malin, 'Puck Fair 1956 Will Be Remembered', *Kerryman*, 18 August 1956.

131 Brendan Malin, 'The Goat Must Carry Puck on his Ample Back', *Kerryman*, 16 August 1958.

132 John Downing, 'Pa Houlihan Looks Back on Puck Fair', *Kerryman*, 23 August 1985.

133 Patrick W. Smyth, 'Puck Fair Through the Eyes of the Bridge', *Kerryman*, 5 August 1961.

134 P.W. Smyth, 'Puck Fair is an Event Unique Throughout World', *Kerryman*, 8 August 1959.

135 P.W. Smyth, 'Puck Programme to be Changed in 1960?', *Kerryman*, 15 August 1959.

136 'Puck Fair to be Filmed this Year', *Kerryman*, 4 June 1960.

137 Maurice F. O'Leary, 'Puck Fair in Full Blast', *Kerryman*, 13 August 1960.

138 'But Cash is Short', *Irish Independent*, 4 July 1961.

139 Eric G.E. Zuelow, *Making Ireland Irish: Tourism and National Identity Since the Irish Civil War* (Syracuse University Press, New York, 2009) page 124.

140 'New Secretary of Puck Fair will be Paid', *Kerryman*, 21 November 1964.

141 'Puck Fair: An Urgent Appeal', *Kerryman*, May 23, 1959.

142 'New Secretary of Puck Fair will be Paid', *Kerryman*, 21 November 1964.

143 'Puck Fair', *Irish Press*, 25 February 1967.

6

PUCK FAIR IN MODERN TIMES

By 1970, the programme of events at Puck Fair had to be curtailed due to insufficient funding, and in 1973, in response to poor attendances at organising meetings, the committee threatened to quit.[1] At a later meeting, most of the committee carried out their threat and resigned en masse. In an effort to find people to run the fair, a public meeting was called in Killorglin, and the Laune Rangers GAA club was invited to attend, as potential new organisers. The event was handed over to the club, whose chairman Jimmy Coffey commented, 'We felt that somebody should uphold the tradition'. The development divided opinion in the town, but one shopkeeper concluded, 'There was no one else to run it'.[2] The *Kerryman* commented:

> What a tragedy it would have been had there been no Puck Fair in Killorglin in 1974 – and how perilously close that tragedy was. Had it not been for Jimmy Coffey and his band of merry helpers one of the greatest traditional fairs in Ireland – indeed in the view of some in the world – would have died a quiet death, to live only in the minds of those lucky enough to have been present at one time or another.[3]

The club envisaged their first fair, financially, as a break-even operation,[4] but ultimately they hoped that revenue from the event could be used for the benefit of the club, in particular towards the building of a sports centre.[5] This was an ambitious conception, given that no admission charge was collected from visitors, that the former committees had trouble raising sufficient money from local traders, and that they were taking on the former organisers' debts (although the latter were then modest). In addition, Bord Fáilte continued to decline financial assistance,[6] and although some income came from donations by sponsors such as Guinness, this had already been complained of as being too small.[7]

Laune Rangers ran the fair again in 1975, but found that the costs of staging the event had risen significantly, while the subscriptions from the town had remained static.[8] Afterwards, officers of the club realised that the financial return to it was too meagre and that it's other activities had become neglected, and so they decided to bow out.[9]

For the fair of 1976 an emergency meeting of Killorglin's Community Council was called, and a new committee was hastily assembled.[10] In the following year, only after 'a last effort' to get local people interested was the event organised.[11] After the fair of 1978, committee spokesperson Mary Clifford revealed that 'This year we got a feedback from Killorglin people that they're just not interested anymore'. She said she would be 'very, very sad' if that was to mean the end of the fair.[12] 'Was this the last Puck?', wondered the *Kerryman*.

Up to 60,000 people continued to attend the fair, and a quarter of a million pounds could be spent in local bars and shops.[13] Nevertheless, local apathy about the event may have formed, as it brought inconveniences as well as benefits: there were parking difficulties and shops were less accessible. Every morning a large amount of litter covered the streets; Jimmy Coffey noted after the fair of 1974, 'The streets were in an appalling condition ... and we had quite a lot of complaint from the residents'.[14] Some locals did not like the arrival of Travellers when they came in large numbers. By the mid-1970s the Travellers had switched their traditional wooden caravans for modern steel caravans pulled by car. At the fair of 1978, a businessman said that there were about 6,000 travelling people in Killorglin from the North and England at the event: 'They virtually took over the town and caused a lot of damage to local property. They parked their big caravans in local meadows with their horses and broke down a lot of gates and doors', he added. Organising committee chairman, Mr Tom Moriarty said that he had to take 'a lot of stick' from local people.[15]

In 1979, a former chairman of the committee pinpointed another reason for the decline in local enthusiasm: 'Killorglin used to depend on Puck for business. Now with three factories and an extended tourist season, the town is busy without the Fair'.[16]

THE FAIRS OF THE 1970S

Problems aside, the fairs of the 1970s had their own character. English hippies were first noted at the fair in 1969.[17] 'In the early '70s,' recalled local woman Anne Lucey, many years later, 'Puck was hippies with long hair selling leather wrist bands, woven belts and love beads and stinking of patchouli oil in the bright packed stalls'.[18] Of the fair of 1977, a visiting reporter wrote, 'Mixed in among the travelling people's stalls (the backbone of Puck for years) were hippies selling leather armlets, necklaces and earrings, reading the Tarots, and Indian traders marketing jeans and cheesecloth blouses with their usual energy'.[19]

The tricksters were still around. Roulette, the Three Card Trick, Wheel of Fortune and Trick o' the Loop were still being played on the streets.[20] In 1977, a man from Kildare, who said he had been coming to Puck Fair for thirty-five years, was arrested for operating a roulette table. A Castlemaine man told Gardaí how he had lost some money on the game, borrowed £5 from his wife, bet it on black and won, after which the operator walked away without paying out. A scuffle broke out between them, and Gardaí later found the offender hiding behind a van.[21] At the same fair, journalist Nell McCafferty observed a backpacker confidently wage £10 on a card with a Three Card Trick man, only to lose it instantly and watch dumbfounded as the miscreants made their escape.[22]

Remarkably, there were still some Travellers engaging in 'tangling' for a few pounds at the fair. McCafferty watched as a tangler joined two farmers, who turned out to be neighbours, forcing the pair's palms together to seal the deal.[23] In general, however, fortunes had improved for the Travellers, as Donal Hickey reported for the *Cork Examiner*: 'Locals were amazed at the apparent prosperity of yesterday's travelling people who arrived in £5,000 caravans, Volvos and Rovers. Some came from England and from cross-border markets. Others bade a speedy fare-

Parading in Celtic style, 1984. (© David Hurn. Courtesy of Magnum Photos)

well to Killorglin when a rumour went out that the customs and excise officials were in town.[24]

There was no longer any mention of impromptu ballad-singing on the streets during the 1970s, and the tradition appears to have ceased. The custom of visiting singers and musicians performing at the puck stand also faded, and in the middle of the decade one of the organisers admitted that the practice had been allowed to die off for the past few years.[25]

In 1976, Patrick Houlihan set up an exhibition about the history of Puck Fair, and for many years he showed old photographs, newspaper cuttings and memorabilia.[26] Included was the stitched tricolour which had been flown from the puck stand in defiance of the RIC at the fair of 1920.[27]

If some aspects of the fair faded, the goat ceremony was not one of them. A new development during the decade was the 'Lady of the Laune' competition, which began in 1972. It may have been inspired by the Rose of Tralee. Local heats were held in a handful of locations throughout Kerry after which a young woman was chosen to take part in the goat ceremony. The role of the Lady of the Laune took place within an expanded setting of the parade as a colourful pageant inspired by the mythological era of the Fianna. In 1972, six young men on horseback headed the parade, while two others led Irish wolfhounds, and another pair carried falcons on their arms.[28] Notably, on this occasion, the Lady replaced the girl-queen, and it was she who crowned the goat; this was done with a new crown, again made of copper.[29]

At the night-time dethronement that year:

> The goat was taken from his perch at 10 o'clock on Saturday night and nearly lost his beard in the parade that followed. Flames from a pair of torches at the back of Joe O'Shea's truck were fanned by a breeze and the king – relieved of his crown a short time previously by the Lady of the Laune – had to get down almost on his haunches.[30]

The Fianna presentation was expanded further over the following years. In 1973, horses drew two of the floats through the parade; and three years later there were twelve Fianna horsemen and twenty-four footsoldiers.[31] After 1979 the role of Lady of the Laune was dropped.[32]

A new tradition was established in 1976, when for the first time the girl-queen addressed the crowd, in Irish and English, welcoming them to the fair and giving visitors the freedom of the town.[33] This proclamation has remained a feature of the ceremony to this day.

Selling animals outside the Oisin Cinema, Langford Street, 1983. (© Martin Parr. Courtesy of Magnum Photos)

The question of whether the goat for the ceremony was caught in the wild during the 1970s, can no more be answered definitively than it can be for the previous decade. In 1976 there was reported to have been a five-hour goat chase involving forty people,[34] while a year later the *Sunday Independent* reported that the goat was simply hired for the occasion from a named individual.[35]

In 1971 there were twenty-eight pubs operating in the town (when 60,000 gallons of beer were said to be consumed for the duration).[36] Drunken escapades continued, with a man in 1973 throwing a 'No Parking' sign into the Laune 'just to see if it would sink'. ('Unfortunately it must have because it has not been recovered yet', commented the Garda Superintendent.)[37] The one-hour closing period enforced in the 1960s was extended to a three-hour break between 3 a.m. and 6 a.m., but in 1976 Puck Fair could still be characterised as 'an occasion for heroic, non-stop drinking'.[38] Two years later, Donal Hickey attended the fair, which was washed out by heavy rain:

> Hawkers' stands were deserted and it was strictly a day for the pubs, which opened at 6 a.m. after a three-hour break. By early afternoon, several drunken figures could be seen tottering along the footpaths and stumbling under stalls for cover. One intoxicated man dragged himself from a doorway and asked a Garda what time it was. 'Half past Eight' replied the officer. 'Morning or night' retorted the drunken reveller.[39]

Re-branding Puck Fair

The fair was rescued from the possibility of extinction by the committee formed in 1979, which initiated a five-year development plan.[40] Chairman Dermot Foley later commented, 'Our main aim was to change the fair's image from a drunkard's paradise, to a family carnival, where parents could bring children without having to worry'.[41] In the same year, the committee approached the organisers of two other old traditional fairs, Ballycastle Old Lammas Fair, County Antrim, and Ballinasloe Horse Fair, County Galway, to learn from each about improving standards and generating new ideas for their events.[42] This initiative bore further fruit when Bord Fáilte became involved in 1981, producing a colour brochure on all three fairs, in co-operation with the Northern Ireland Tourist Board.[43] From the 1980s the committee concentrated on providing an ever greater range of entertainment, more diversions for children, more street stalls, and more car-parking facilities.[44] 'I am satisfied that it will go on,' Dermot Foley was able to comment in 1983, 'Puck fair is important to our community. It is commercially valuable and there is a spin-off for everybody. It's in the interest of everybody that the tradition of the Fair should be maintained'.[45]

The ballad singers of old no longer appeared at Puck Fair, and a large part of the committee's development plans revolved around bringing music and song back into the event. A regular busking competition was begun in 1984,[46] which they praised a year later because it had 'put the music back on the streets'.[47] One regular busker was a man who styled himself Señor John Maher, from Athy in County Kildare; he wore a Mexican hat and a poncho and Cuban-heeled boots, and said he had been coming to the fair since 1944.[48] Contemporary rock and pop acts started to be presented in 1987, and such free music events have continued to be a major attraction for night-time crowds.

The ceremony of the crowning of the goat remained clothed in the imagery of the Fianna. The crown was stolen in 1988, but a replacement was donated the following year by regular Irish-American visitor, Silky Sullivan, from Memphis, Tennessee, who had a $5,000 jewelled crown made by craftsmen from his home town.[49]

Local enthusiasm for the fair was revived so successfully that by 1991 long-serving committee member Declan Mangan was able to say of the town's business community, 'Everybody is nearly ready and waiting to hand over the cheques'.[50] Two years later, an accumulated debt of £30,000 was reduced to £5,000.[51]

Part of the price for turning Puck Fair into a successful carnival, however, was that the traditional fair element lost its central status. In any case, with the advent of modern cattle marts in most towns, where animals where sold by auction, the traditional method of selling, with two individuals haggling, had passed, and fairs like Puck Fair were no longer significant as cattle fairs. In 1986, the cattle which had long been displayed at the fair field and on the streets of the town were confined to Market Road.[52]

In 2002, the horse fair was removed to Evans' Field, out of the town and across the river at the Tralee Road.[53] That was a big break with tradition, and a regular visitor complained, 'Taking the horse fair out is a mistake. It spoils the atmosphere'.[54]

Nevertheless, Puck Fair had re-invented itself and secured a future. Afterwards, its importance was celebrated in a number of ways. In 1998 An Post issued a Puck Fair stamp, and Bord Fáilte distributed several thousand colour brochures promoting the festival.[55] In the following year, Michael Houlihan, grandson of Michael, and son of Patrick Houlihan, published the first history of the event, *Puck Fair History and Traditions*.[56] In 2001, under a community initiative, and funded by a government grant, a bronze statue of a puck goat, an impressive one and a half times life size, designed by Valentia Island sculptor Alan Ryan-Hall, was unveiled, mounted high on a large boulder at the Laune Bridge entrance to the town.[57] These were all signs that Puck Fair was here to stay.

The coloured lanterns that used to illuminate the Puck stand in the 1870s have long gone. But a spectacular fireworks display has taken place on the last night of every fair for the past few years. Huge crowds gather along the bridge and on the hill slope of Lower Bridge Street to view the spectacle, the flashing light show reflected in the dark, slow-moving waters of the river below. Afterwards, sated crowds move slowly back up the town. Puck Fair is over – passed for another year – but there will always be another.

Notes

1 'Killorglin', *Kerryman*, 3 July 1971; 'Puck Fair Committee Threaten to Resign', *Kerryman*, 30 June 1973.
2 Eamon Horan, 'Rangers to Run Puck', *Kerryman*, 24 May 1974.
3 'GAA Club Involved for First Time', *Kerryman*, 9 August 1974.
4 'Big Plans for Expansion in 1975', *Kerryman*, 9 August 1974.
5 Michael Hilliard, 'Puck Fair Time Again', *Kerryman*, 8 August 1975.
6 'Puck to go International', *Kerryman*, 16 August 1974.
7 'Puck Fair', *Kerryman*, 26 May 1973.
8 Michael Hilliard, 'Puck Fair Time Again', *Kerryman*, 8 August 1975.
9 'Big Crowds But Less Money at Puck Fair', *Kerryman*, 15 August 1975; 'Laune Rangers Criticise RTE', *Kerryman*, 23 January 1976.
10 Ian O'Leary, 'Tradition That Can't Be Killed', *Kerryman*, 6 August 1976.
11 'Life in King Puck', *Irish Press*, 10 March 1977; 'Brutality, Small Schools and the Killorglin Puck Fair', *Irish Times*, 21 February 1977.

12 'Was this the Last Puck?', *Kerryman*, 18 August 1978.

13 Seamus Counihan, 'Puck Fair to be Dropped?', *Irish Press*, 14 August 1978.

14 'Puck to go International', *Kerryman*, 16 August 1974.

15 Seamus Counihan, 'Puck Fair to be Dropped?', *Irish Press*, 14 August 1978.

16 'Duffy tries his Luck', *Irish Press*, 14 August 1979.

17 Tony Meade, 'Puck Still Holds its Pull', *Kerryman*, 16 August 1969.

18 Anne Lucey, 'Timeless Puck Measures a Changing Life', *Kerryman*, 6 August 1993.

19 Rosita Sweetman, 'King Puck Had a 3-day Warm-Up', *Sunday Independent*, 14 August 1977.

20 'GAA Club Involved for First Time', *Kerryman*, 9 August 1974; Dick Grogan, 'An Occasion for Heroic Drinking', *Irish Times*, 11 August 1976; Nell McCafferty, 'King Puck Looked Down on Frantic Scene of People, Cattle and Dung', *Irish Times*, 12 August 1977.

21 'Scuffle at Roulette', *Kerryman*, 16 September 1977.

22 Nell McCafferty, 'King Puck Looked Down on Frantic Scene of People, Cattle and Dung', *Irish Times*, 12 August 1977.

23 *Ibid.*

24 Donal Hickey, 'Puck Washed Out, But Not Dry', *Cork Examiner*, 12 August 1978.

25 Ian O'Leary, 'Tradition That Can't be Killed', *Kerryman*, 6 August 1976.

26 'Tradition That Can't be Killed', *Kerryman*, 6 August 1976.

27 'Puck Fair Display Opens', *Kerryman*, 4 August 1979; 'Pa Houlihan's Puck Museum', *Kerryman*, 5 August 1983.

28 Ian O'Leary, 'Eight Days of Puck This Year', *Kerryman*, 5 August 1972.

29 'Days of the Fianna at Puck Fair', *Irish Press*, 11 August 1972.

30 'Puck Men Out With Brushes and Shovels', *Kerryman*, 19 August 1972.

31 'Records Should be Broken at Puck Fair', *Kerryman*, 11 August 1973; Ian O'Leary, 'Tradition That Can't be Killed', *Kerryman*, 6 August 1976.

32 Advertisement for the CYMS Killorglin mentions the Lady of the Laune Competition, *Kerryman*, 13 July 1979.

33 Ian O'Leary, 'Thongs Greet Enthronement of King Puck', *Kerryman*, 13 August 1976.

34 'Gotta Get a Goat!', *Kerryman*, 6 August 1976.

35 Rosita Sweetman, 'King Puck Had a 3-day Warm-Up', *Sunday Independent*, 14 August 1977.

36 Noel Smith, 'King Puck May Not Get US Trip', *Sunday Independent*, 8 August 1971.

37 'Threw road sign into the Laune', *Kerryman*, 22 September 1973.

38 'Puck Fair Finally Gets The Goat', *Irish Press*, 10 August 1976; T J Barrington, *Discovering Kerry* (Blackwater Press, Dublin, 1976) page 228.

39 Donal Hickey, 'Puck Washed Out, But Not Dry', *Cork Examiner*, 12 August 1978.

40 'Even King Puck Could Not Hold Off The Rain', *Irish Independent*, 13 August 1980.

41 Des Cahill, 'Puck Crowned and the Deficit to Drop', *Kerryman*, 14 August 1981.

42 'King Puck for Old Lamas Fair', *Kerryman*, 29 June 1979; 'Treating the King with due respect', *Kerryman*, 7 August 1981.

43 'Treating the King with Due Respect', *Kerryman*, 7 August 1981.

44 'Puck Fair – There's More Entertainment This Year', *Kerryman*, 6 August 1982.

45 'Wednesday is Gathering Day', *Kerryman*, 5 August 1983.

46 'Programme Starts at 7 am on Friday!', *Kerryman*, 10 August 1984.

47 'Plenty of Fun Planned for Puck on this Weekend', *Kerryman*, 9 August 1985.

48 Dan Collins, 'King Puck – the Unwilling Abdicator', *Cork Examiner*, 13 August 1986.

49 Breda Joy, 'Long Wait for the Puck', *Kerryman*, 18 August 1989; Annemaria McEneaney, 'Elusive King Puck Caught Just in Time to Save Festival', *Irish Independent*, 11 August 1992; Breda Joy, 'Acting the Goat as King Puck Reigns Over the Fair', *Kerryman*, 18 August 1995.

50 'Nightmare of Covering the Cost', *Kerryman*, 9 August 1991.

51 Noel Twomey, 'Puck Fair Grows in Stature', *Kerryman*, 6 August 1993.

52 Breda Joy, 'Gathering and Crowning in Killorglin on Sunday', *Kerryman*, 8 August 1986.

53 'Puck is a Carnival for the People', *Kerryman*, 1 August 2002.

54 Anne Lucey, 'Crowds Fill Streets as Horse Fair Moves Across the River', *Kerryman*, 15 August 2002.

55 'Stamp of approval for Puck Fair', *Kerryman*, 5 June 1998.

56 Michael Houlihan, *Puck Fair History and Traditions* (Treaty Press, Limerick, 1999).

57 Emer Connolly, 'Killorglin to Cast King Puck in Bronze for Millennium', *Kerryman*, 30 June 2000; Emer Connolly, 'Puck Sculpture to be Unveiled', *Kerryman*, 12 July 2001; Donal O'Reilly, 'Puck to be Cast in Bronze', *Kerryman*, 8 March 2001.

APPENDIX I

Early Origin Stories about the Puck Ceremony

The following collection of stories show what were thought to be the origins of the goat ceremony of Puck Fair in the hundred years after it was first noticed in print by the *Topographical Dictionary of Ireland* in 1837.

The Earliest Stories

The earliest explanations for the goat ceremony were published in a report of the fair by the *Cork Examiner* in 1846, in which the writer said that the goat ritual was an 'ancient custom, which was at one time sacrilege, or cowardice to neglect'.[1]

The report began by saying that the event was called Puck Fair on account of its being a great market for goats, 'and, in order to pay a marked tribute of respect to that hardy race, a fatherly, sage looking mountain chieftain, antlered and bearded, is selected and adorned with the most grotesque finery'.

There was, however, a second explanation for the ritual. The shape of a side-saddle was sometimes created upon the goat's back, 'intended it is said, for the first farmers daughter who "went out" – was married – as an encouragement to future aspirants'. This explanation appears to mean that the goat ceremony was a kind of celebration of the marriage ritual; perhaps a goat was a traditional marriage gift, or formed a common part of a young countrywoman's dowry.

Thirdly, the custom of faction fighting was mentioned: one faction 'made "Puck" a signal of defiance, and over his devoted head was the battle waged with barbarous impetuosity'. The writer went on to refer to the goat as 'the outlawed animal', so the goat may have been a mascot for one of the factions, although this was not made explicit in the report. (As the account of the *Cork Examiner* forms the earliest explanation for the goat ceremony, it is reproduced in full in the third appendix to the present book.)

The Story of the Conways and the Goat

In 1861, the Killorglin correspondent of the *Tralee Chronicle* recounted that two goats were displayed that year. One was placed in the centre of the town, and the other on one of the last remaining towers of the Blennerhassett mansion, 'where centuries ago the ancestors of "The Conway O'Connor" – (last of his race) would prevent a goat from desecrating their home'.[2] (The Conway-O'Connor family of north Kerry had married into the female line of the original family of Castle Conway some time after 1660.)[3] This scenario appears to suggest that the public display of the goat was a kind of sardonic commentary upon the manners of the Conways.

The Story of the Cromwellian Soldiers and the Goat

In 1886, Killorglin priest Fr Thomas Lawlor travelled among the Irish-American community to raise funds for the construction of a new Catholic church for the town. He told a journalist from the *Chicago Herald* about the prospect of evictions of tenants, of the progress of Home Rule for Ireland, and of rack-renting landlords. He also relayed the origin of Puck Fair, as summarised by the journalist:

> In the noted little village is annually held the celebrated Puck Fair. Tradition gives this version of the reason which led to this annual gathering … When a party of Cromwell's troopers made a raid into Kerry the goats that were browsing on Carran Tual were alarmed by the approach of the English minions whose arms glistened in the sun, rushed down the hillsides and ran wildly through the town. This unusual spectacle aroused the people, and being informed of the cause of it by their scouts, who did not reach the town until some time after the goats, they prepared to meet the enemy. Their heroic resistance to the band of well-drilled soldiers is

recorded in Irish song and story, and the goats that warned the people of their danger are commemorated by the holding of a fair annually … The story of how 'Killorglin was saved' is related many a time, and a representation of a goat is conspicuously displayed on the crumbling walls of the ruined castle.[4]

This 'tradition', which was 'recorded in Irish song and story', cannot have been very strong, if indeed it existed: in 1894, the writer of an account of Puck Fair was able to assert that 'The origin of this curious custom is not known … and there seems to be no tradition relating to it among the peasantry'.[5] Fr Lawlor's story may have been an attempt to stir up some patriotic fervour and encourage the flow of financial donations by mentioning Cromwell, the arch-enemy of the Irish.

In any case, the Cromwellian source for the goat celebration is unlikely to be true. In 1652, Cromwellian soldiers did indeed appear at Killorglin, by sea, from a ship which had been sent to carry men and materials for the creation of a number of small boats, which were to be used later for the siege of Ross Castle, at Lough Lein, near Killarney. These boats were apparently dragged back up the Laune River to the lake to mount a water-side attack upon the castle, to which all the remaining Irish forces had retreated. Once they were spotted on the water, the Irish surrendered, reputedly because they were familiar with a prophecy that Ross Castle could only be captured from the water. A herd of goats may have disturbed the residents of Killorglin, who may have fled the soldiers, but no celebration of any such incident can have taken place afterwards. Killorglin's resident landlords, the Blennerhassetts, were supporters of the Cromwellian cause. Towards the end of 1651 and into 1652, Castle Conway appears to have been under the command of Robert Blennerhassett, listed in documents as 'Captain Hassett'.[6] He had served against the Irish in 1649 (and possibly earlier) and then joined the Cromwellian forces. He was married to (or later married) Avis, a daughter of Edward Conway, and thus inherited Conway Castle and its estate. As former Cromwellians, and as the owners of Killorglin's August fair, the Blennerhassets would not have tolerated a goat display at the fair based upon such an incident; and after the family departed the castle in 1795, it is unlikely that a ceremony developed in the years afterwards based on an event that was supposed to have occurred 150 years previously.

The Story of How Only One Goat was Brought to the Fair

The next story to be advanced was that the goat display commemorated the first ever occasion of the fair, when a single goat was brought in for sale. In 1894, an anonymous article in the *Irish Monthly* concluded, 'It may be, as some say, that in old days when it was proposed to hold a fair in Killorglin, the first, and perhaps, the only animal brought in was a goat'.

In 1900, the *Strand Magazine*, of London, reproduced a photograph of the goat at the Puck stand taken by a Dublin reader, who most likely conveyed the information printed about the fair. The origin of the custom, 'founded on fact', it said, dated from the middle of the eighteenth century:

> The story is this: Some persons wished to start a fair in opposition to a neighbouring one; the start was apparently a very bad one, as the only animal presented for sale was a Billy-goat. The committee, nothing daunted, bought the animal, and, at the suggestion of some sage in their midst, held him over till the anniversary, when they placed him in a position similar to that which his worthy and venerable successor holds in the photograph.[7]

A year later, the correspondent of the *Kerry Sentinel* stated, 'The origin of how this fair came to have its present cognomen[8] is involved in a haze of mystery; but the most accepted opinion appears to be that at its first inception the only four-footed beast offered for sale was a puck goat'.[9]

The Story of the Goat Representing the Fair

Some time around the year 1900, a pseudonymous letter written to the *Kerry Sentinel* stated that the goat display was first established in the early 1800s.[10] A resident gentleman of the area proposed that a fair be established in Killorglin, but that it would commence in an area called 'New Town' or 'New Killorglin'. This was where the poorer people of the town, probably casual labourers and their families, lived, and the event was conceived as a kind of boon for that district. These homes appear to have lain at the bottom of Lower Bridge Street, near the river bank. The letter was summarised by Anthony Walsh in a later article on the origins of the event:

> In 1806 the establishing of the new fair was published and six months after the committee met to discuss the name of the fair. It was then pro-

posed that a bonham,[11] calf and goat should be placed on a raised platform in a conspicuous place, but the committee disagreed as the trouble of hoisting these three animals was too much. Therefore they agreed that the Puck would be the most picturesque as he was also King of the mountain animals and the parish of New Killorglin so poor that the goat was the commonest and most highly prized animal at that time.

The first fair was not well attended while the goat was in his crib on a platform about ten feet high and a green flag waving over his head.[12]

The fair of 1807 was supposedly a great improvement, and for the 1808 event the committee met on 1 July and decided to have the goat even better presented at the coming fair;

… so they agreed to subscribe, but not having enough, went about the country and in some places were offered potatoes, cabbages, etc., which they sold and the money was used for the proper rigging out of the Goat. They also employed a few good pipers and other musicians who were placed beside the Puck and beside them again were two buckets of poteen[13], flanked by a couple of dozen yellow meal cakes[14], while about the Puck's throne floated the flags of all nations under the Green Flag, the old zig-zag poles were hung with mountain heather and slogans and greetings such as Eireann go bragh,[15] 'Welcome to all', 'Hail for the Mountain Prince', were displayed in various places on the scaffolding.

The third day of the fair ended with the goat being let down with a rope and covered with green cloth; then a youth dressed in a red coat and a high hat covered with heather led him about the fair, headed by musicians and the highest gentlemen in the place, the whole scene being one of enjoyment and merriment.

This story appeared in around 1900, yet in 1909, the Killorglin correspondent of the *Kerryman* wrote that, 'Puck Fair has been going on from year to year in Killorglin for such a long period that nobody seems to know when or how it originated'.[16] The details are also contradicted by a newspaper report from 1841, which observed that it was in that year that the goat was first raised up high for display, as opposed to being paraded on the ground.[17]

The Story of the Goat as a Figurehead for the Fair
In 1912, the Killorglin correspondent of the *Kerry Sentinel* wrote that:

> The origin of this practice is not easy to trace, because it seems to have arisen, like many other traditions, out of small beginnings. The most feasible account gleaned from that celebrated individual, 'the oldest inhabitant', seems to be that some time about the year 1820 there used to be a goat fair held in Killorglin, which at that time consisted of only a few thatched cabins ... thousands of these useful little animals found their way on the 11th of August each year to the village of Killorglin ...
>
> There was then a gentleman named Blennerhassett living at Castleconway, in the neighbourhood, and he, with the village folk, succeeded in getting a patent for holding a general fair on the 11th August, all agreeing that a puck goat was the most natural and appropriate sign by which the fair would in future be known.[18]

This story was contradicted the following year, when the newspaper repeated the story from 1886 about the goats warning of the approach of Cromwellian soldiers.[19]

The Story that the Goat Display was Brought from Kilgobnet
A second origin story published in 1912, linked the establishment of the goat display with a fair at the nearby village of Kilgobnet.

> One legend has it that the fair was first held not in Killorglin but in the village of Kilgobnet, and that on one occasion the guns of Cromwell's soldiers in West Carberry frightened the goats in the mountains of Mangerton, Toomies and the Reeks, with the result that the startled animals rushed into the village of Kilgobnet, where a fair was being held. The villagers surrounded the goats and sold them at the fair. But the visitation was of twofold value: it also warned the people of the approach of the Cromwellian soldiers, and – so the story finishes – in gratitude to the goat family they elected a 'Puck' King of the Fair.[20]

In 1917, Edward Twiss, of Kilmacow, County Kilkenny, wrote to the *Irish Times*, stating that Puck Fair had a connection with Kilgobnet. He linked it to an attempt to control the custom of faction fighting during the 1820s and '30s.

> Some 80 or 90 years ago, the gathering which represented Puck Fair, as now held in the town of Killorglin, was held at a place some few miles outside the town.
>
> Though nominally a fair, this annual gathering was chiefly held to give rival factions an opportunity of meeting and indulging in the then national pastime of faction-fighting: the result invariably being a large crop of broken heads and bodies more or less damaged. This at length caused the local authorities charged with maintenance of the peace so much trouble, that they issued an edict that, in future, the fair should be held in the town of Killorglin, hoping in this way to control more effectively the lawless element. This element, however, decided that it would not be thus deprived of its annual gala, and refused en masse to come to Killorglin on the appointed day. It insisted instead on going to the old happy hunting ground, and indulging therein in the time-honoured revelry – all except one old man, who led a solitary puck goat for sale to the town of Killorglin.
>
> In derision, this poor animal was seized, placed on a platform in the centre of the town, and bells were tied to its long horns – an ordeal which some representative of the male goat species has to submit to on every 11th August to the present day.[21]

Mr Twiss said he obtained this information 'from a thoroughly trustworthy source some years ago'. (He may have heard it through family connections with Kerry; there was a Twiss family in Kerry from at least the 1700s, who lived on land originally granted to the Blennerhassetts, near Castleisland, and a daughter of the family was married to Arthur Blennerhassett (d. 1815) of Ballyseedy, near Tralee.)[22]

Father Quinlan's Story
In 1925, Fr John Quinlan of Killarney told the following story of the origin of Puck Fair to a journalist with the *Kerry Reporter*. 'This view I gathered as a child from my mother', he explained:

An old penal law directed against the Catholic body compelled them to sell their livestock to the Ascendancy[23] at fixed prices ... Jenkyn Conway, who got Killorglin and district as a grant, was a cute, canny Welshman – he knew that his tenure of the land might be insecure, so he set himself to line his pocket well by stock-jobbing.[24] He had plenty of willing satellites to support his ventures, and so a series of compulsory markets was established in the district.

Nor must we forget that Jenkyn Conway and his gang of adventurers held the native Irish and their religion in the utmost contempt. Imbued with that Satanic cunning of theirs they selected the goat – and old emblem of anti-Christ to preside over these compulsory markets thus signalising their double purpose – robbery of the people by law and contempt of their law-prescribed[25] religion. [26]

The Story of the Goat and the Tithe War

In 1928, it was asserted by Batt Dwyer, Killorglin District Court Clerk, and Thomas T. Foley, the Baron of the Fair, that the campaign against the collection of Church tithes had been the origin of the goat ceremony.

Between 1831 and 1836, a campaign of resistance was waged by Catholic tillage farmers against the imposition of tithes. Payment consisted of 10 per cent of the value of a farmer's agricultural produce, which was often paid in livestock.

Mr Dwyer states that the people of Killorglin district, with those of every Catholic district in the country resisted to the fullest the imposition of the Protestant Tithe tax, whereupon the tithe-gatherers and bailiffs swept their stock from the mountains.

After a big 'round up' the bailiffs arrived one evening at the ford where Killorglin's substantial bridge now stands. While endeavouring to force a large seizure of mixed animals across the river, a huge 'Puck' goat broke away and naturally faced back up the mountain. His example was quickly followed by the rest of the herd, and the bailiffs, being too exhausted after a long, hard day's work to attempt a recapture, resumed their journey to Tralee with but a meagre haul from the people of Killorglin.

It was a 'Puck' goat that defeated the seizure, and in fitting celebration of this achievement, the most presentable representatives of the species, on each anniversary day, was bedecked and beribboned and hauled to the top of Castle Conway.[27]

If this incident took place during the 1830s, it is difficult to understand why the story was not well circulated and commonly understood in the following years.

Conclusion

Clearly, there was no single well-known tradition concerning the goat element, if these theories, each at such variance with the others, were suggested over the period of 100 years or so since Puck Fair was known to have been established. Joseph O'Connor, who attended his first Puck Fair in 1905, said later, 'No one can tell with certainty how and when the legend of the puck goat came into circulation. Folklore – that is, *bona-fide* Gaelic folkore of more than a hundred years' tradition – knows nothing about it, and literature in prose and poetry of equal vintage knows less'.[28]

Notes

1 'Puck Fair', *Cork Examiner*, 17 August 1846.
2 'Puck Fair – Yesterday', *Tralee Chronicle*, 13 August 1861.
3 John D'Alton, *King James's Irish Army List, Volume 2* (John Russell Smith, London, 1890 [1689]) page 374.
4 'How the Goats Saved Killorglin. The Origin of Puck Fair. Father Lawlor Seeking Aid for a Poverty-Stricken People', *Kerry Sentinel*, 19 November 1886. Article reprinted from the *Chicago Herald*.
5 M.C.K., 'Puck Fair', *Irish Monthly*, Vol. 22, July 1894, page 375.
6 See 'Extract from a MS History of the County of Kerry, in the Library of the Royal Irish Academy', reproduced in Caesar Otway, *Sketches in Ireland* (William Curry, Dublin, 1839) pages 380-381.
7 'The Billy-Goat of Puck Fair', *Strand Magazine*, Vol. 19, May 1900.
8 cognomen = name, title.
9 'Puck Fair', *Kerry Sentinel*, 17 August 1901.
10 The letter was signed by one 'Centurian and Patriot', 'Centurian' probably intended to mean Centurion, a soldier (although it might have been a mistaken rendering for Centenarian, to indicate a person 100 years old, or of advanced age).
11 A young pig.
12 Anthony Walsh, 'The Origin of Puck Fair' in *The Irishman's Annual* (Michael Glazier, Tralee, 1955) page 58.
13 *Poitín*: the traditional Irish white spirit drink, with a high alcohol content.
14 'yellow meal cakes': slices of plain, coarse flatbread.
15 *Erin go Bragh*: 'Ireland forever'.

16 'Pars From Puck', *Kerryman*, 21 August 1909.
17 'Puck Fair', *Kerry Evening Post*, 11 August 1841.
18 'Killorglin (Puck) Fair', *Kerry Sentinel*, 21 August 1912. This extract has here been divided into paragraphs.
19 'Puck Fair', *Kerry Sentinel*, 16 August 1913.
20 'Puck Fair', *Connaught Telegraph*, 10 August 1912.
21 Letter to the *Irish Times*, 22 June 1917 by Mr Edward Twiss, Kilmacow, County Kilkenny.
22 Valerie Bary, *Houses of Kerry* (Ballinakella Press, County Clare, 1994) pages 15 and 154.
23 The Irish ruling elite, who comprised Protestant landowners, clergy and higher professionals.
24 Dealing in livestock.
25 Law-*proscribed*. i.e. outlawed.
26 'Origin of 'Puck'', *Kerry Reporter*, 15 August 1925.
27 'At the Fair of Puck', *Kerry Reporter*, 18 August 1928.
28 Joseph O'Connor, 'King Puck Was Never a Hero', *Irish Times*, 9 August 1955.

Appendix II

Later Origin Stories about the Puck Ceremony

The Story of Saint Patrick and the Goat
Liam Foley, writing in the *Kerryman* in 1945, told a story of St Patrick (although tradition states that the Saint got no nearer to Kerry than Knockpatrick, County Limerick, in AD 448).

> It seems that in the course of his itinerary the Saint had reached the Kerry border. He was depending upon a few goats for a supply of milk. During the night these goats were stolen, and lack of so necessary a provision prevented the Saint from proceeding further. He resolved to detour a community that was so utterly depraved and lacking in hospitality. However, a chieftain from the Barony of Dunkerran saved the day for Kerry. He presented as a gift to the Saint a magnificent Puck-goat and a hundred of the finest goats from his herds on the slopes of the Glencar highlands. The Saint came no further west, but instead of a malediction[1] he gave to Kerry that benediction that will live forever in the salutations of the Irish Race – '*Go mbeannuigh Dia siar sibh*'.[2] Killorglin being the natural centre of defence of the barony of that time has ever since held the Puck-goat in the highest esteem, and elevated him to the place of honour for three days each year.[3]

The Story of the Goat who Fought the Vikings

The famous English anthropologist Margaret Murray (d. 1963) visited Puck Fair in August 1952, when she and her two companions, Miss Anne Baker and Miss Olga Tufnell, were told a single origin story – that the goat ceremony owed its beginning to an incident with the Norsemen (also known as the Danes, the Vikings, and, in Irish, Na Lochlannaigh).

> The legend explanatory of the ceremony is that in the 9th or 10th century the Norsemen (here always called Danes) were continually raiding Ireland, massacring and plundering and seeking places to settle themselves. On one occasion a large army of Danes landed on the coast of Kerry, and were marching inland when they met a wild he-goat from the hills, who so terrified them that they fled back to their ships and never ventured to return to that coast again. In memory of that event the crowning of a representative of the victorious animal, who saved the country from disaster, has taken place annually.[4]

This information came from conversations with the locals, which she regarded as definitive. 'It is strongly denied that the ceremony dates to the pre-Christian era. The period of the invasions of the Norse men (9th-10th century) is always insisted upon.'

Encounters with the Vikings were certainly once a feature of ancient Killorglin life. Historian of Killorglin, Kieran Foley, noted that a Viking presence in the Killorglin area was indicated by the traditional story of the building of the roadway, Bóthar na Lochlannach, through the bogs west of Killorglin.[5] T.J. Barrington listed raids in 845 and 857, in north Kerry 'and around the river Laune',[6] while Foley also reported that the writers of the early Irish annals, 'recorded the defeat of a Viking force on the banks of the Laune in 915 AD'.[7]

If this was indeed a well-known, and definitive, tale, it is hard to understand why J.P. O'Sullivan, chairman of the Puck Fair Committee, did not mention it in his survey of the myths and legends of the Killorglin area and of the origin stories of Puck Fair; he wrote in 1951 of a story transmitted to him by the oldest storyteller of the town, that the greatest defeat that the Vikings suffered was at the Laune, but he did not cite a Viking encounter as an origin story for the goat display.[8]

The Story of Daniel O'Connell and the Goat Fair

In the first printed guide to Puck Fair, a booklet written by Michael P. Morris and published in 1958,[9] the writer recounted the story, that in 1808 the landlord of the Killorglin estate was in danger of having his right to collect tolls for the fair abolished by the Lord Lieutenant in Dublin. Supposedly an Act of Parliament empowered the Lord Lieutenant, the head of the British executive in Ireland, to use his discretion as to whether tolls could be collected at cattle, horse and sheep fairs, and the privilege was to be denied. The landlord approached the young Daniel O'Connell, then a rising star as a barrister.

O'Connell is said to have studied the wording of the order against the landlord of Killorglin, and then hit upon the idea of describing the fair as a goat fair only, and thus exempt from the legislation and enabling tolls to continue to be collected. So, as to give weight to the characterisation of the event as a goat fair, a specimen animal was hoisted up to the walls of the castle, where it could be clearly seen and where its physical display bolstered the legal argument. Under this theory, said Morris, the goat was first raised to a platform for the fair of 10 August 1808.

Thomas Mullins, the owner of the Killorglin Castle and estate, and Daniel O'Connell certainly knew and dealt with each other, but it is difficult to believe that Mullins, who was rewarded for supporting the Act of Union of 1800 (abolishing the Irish Parliament and requiring Irish MPs to sit at the British Parliament in London) by being created Baron Ventry in July 1800, subsequently conspired to mislead the authorities in Dublin. Neither do O'Connell's collected letters, and the many biographies of him, mention this story, which would have acted as a wonderful illustration of his legal gifts.

The Story of Lughnasa and a Pagan Origin

An animal is paraded before the people, installed upon a throne, crowned as a king by a young girl and hailed by the assembled crowd, after which a feast of eating and drinking takes place, and the animal is then dethroned. For modern visitors, the basic elements of the goat ceremony can suggest that a religious ritual is taking place, or at least the remnants of one, the purpose of which had been long forgotten.

In 1962, Máire MacNeill published *The Festival of Lughnasa*, a survey of survivals into modern times of the Irish pre-Christian celebration of 1 August. In it, she examined Puck Fair as one such modern survival. The most significant factor encouraging a view of Puck Fair as a once-pagan festival is the central date on which it later took place, 11 August. Before the calendar change of 1752, the fair had been held on 1 August, the date on which the festival of Lughnasa used to be held.

Lughnasa was a celebration dedicated to the Irish god Lugh. He was best known as a skilled warrior and a member of the band of warriors the Tuatha Dé Danann. In one of the stories which circulated about him, after a battle with their enemies, the Formorians, he confronted their king, Breas, who offered to show Lugh, if he spared his life, the proper times to sow, plough and reap. Lugh initiated the first Lughnasa festival, which consisted of feasting and games of strength and skill.

From the 1970s onwards it became a popular theory to link Puck Fair with Lughnasa and paganism. Yet Máire MacNeill in fact concluded that it was unlikely to be a Lughnasa survival. Instead, she noted the Norman history of Killorglin, and suspected that the puck goat had been a fair symbol dating from the Norman period.[10] Certainly, it did not share any of the several elements which her research had identified as deriving from and continuing from the ancient event. These included a tradition of assemblies upon hills and mountains, the lighting of bonfires, the gathering of bilberries, a ritual play or dance to do with Lugh, the sacrifice of a bull, and, following Christianisation, the celebration of a special mass on the last Sunday in July. None of those elements are attached to Killorglin or Puck Fair. Equally, the display of a goat has no parallel in Lughnasa traditions elsewhere. Thoughts of the goat celebration as a pagan event fade further when it is realised that the crowning element appears to date only from the late 1920s,[11] and the role of the girl-queen of the fair from the late 1940s.[12]

The Story of the Norman Fair Display Symbol
In 1962, Máire MacNeill noted that a number of fairs established in rural areas which were once under Norman influence carried an animal as a fair-display symbol. At Mullinavat, County Kilkenny, a fair was held which was also called 'Puck Fair', and at which a male goat was decorated with ribbons, drawn through the fair, and displayed from a height.[13] MacNeill pointed out that the latter fair was held in the Walsh moun-

tains, originally called after the Welsh followers of the Normans, and that it was only nine miles from the Norman town of Waterford, and on the main road to their traditional stronghold of Kilkenny. At the village of Cappawhite, County Tipperary, a white horse, draped in white, was paraded through the fair and installed on top of an ancient Irish fort for the length of the fair. As to their purpose, perhaps such customs began as a way of showing what kind of animal was mostly for sale, or just acted as a prominent visible sign that a fair was on, or were simple emblems or mascots of the fair.

Around 1215, the Normans expanded from north Kerry and established four castles along the line of the River Maine, while two other castles were set up running southwards along the coast, at Callanafersy and at Killorglin. Killorglin castle was probably built by John Fitzthomas (d.1261),[14] or his brother, Maurice. The castle at Killorglin was probably a tower-house. It stood at the brow of the hill overlooking the Laune River.

Patrick Logan commented, 'By the year 1300 the Normans had established fairs and markets in every part of the country where they had control'.[15] A candidate for the founder of a Norman fair at Killorglin is Maurice Fitzthomas Fitzgerald (d.1356), afterwards the 1st Earl of Desmond. On 5 August 1312, Maurice married Katherine de Burgh, daughter of the Earl of Ulster, at Greencastle, County Down, when he was about nineteen years old. Greencastle, situated at the entrance to Carlingford Lough, has been the site of the Ram Fair. A great ram was enthroned on top of the walls of the castle, built by the Normans some-time during the 1230s, where he presided over a three-day fair. This was originally on 1 August; following the calendar change of 1752, the date moved to 12 August. The dates, the duration and the animal ceremony are vividly evocative of Puck Fair. Perhaps Maurice saw the Ram Fair during his stay and later went on to introduce a similar ceremony at Killorglin on the same date. Alternatively, he may have independently established a fair and continued a Norman custom of using animals as fair-display signs, which may have been a more common practice than the few surviving examples suggest.

Maurice was created the 1st Earl of Desmond in 1329, and he and his heirs were allowed to hold their lands in Kerry as a palatinate – as if they were local kings. While in his other territories the crown could give patents for holding fairs and markets, such powers would have been retained by himself and his descendants. We have no evidence for the establishment of a fair at Killorglin, and all the Desmond records were subsequently destroyed, but we do know that Maurice did hold fairs within his lordship generally. He had (or claimed rights over) a market at Adare, County Limerick, and in 1355, as a result of a royal grant, he had a fair and market at Newtown in Olethan, east County Cork.[16]

By the much later time of the Desmond Rebellion (1579-1583), the earldom had fairs at the towns of Rathkeale, Any, and Knockpatrick, all in County Limerick, as itemised in a post-rebellion survey of all the Fitzgeralds' lands and assets, the Desmond Survey. There it was reported that at the fair at Any, Co. Limerick (incidentally, held every 1 and 2 August), Gerald Fitzgerald (d.1583), the 14th Earl of Desmond, had been paid a rent for every stall, a fee for every cow and horse sold, a proportion of the wine and whisky sold, and the value of a tenth part of all the merchandise sold during the two days.[17] Patrick J. O'Connor, in his geographical study of Irish fairs, says that Gerald had a fair at Tralee, 'and his visits to the town were timed to coincide with the fair, when he collected his rents and tolls'.[18]

Unfortunately for the theory of a Norman fair with a goat display symbol at Killorglin, that part of the Desmond Survey which mentions 'Kyllorglan' notes it as a great castle, lists the value of the lands attached to it, and itemises both the fishery of the Laune River and a local rabbit warren – but of a fair there is no mention.[19]

The Story of the Breaking of the Tolls

Paddy O'Sullivan, of Ballybunion, in 1977 recounted that, on the basis of conversations he had held with older people, he believed that there once was an attempt to abolish the collection of tolls by the landlord of Killorglin, although unfortunately he did not date the story to any particular time period.

> When it became known there that tolls were going to be imposed on its fair, both the buyers and sellers and the business people of the town came to the unanimous decision that it would be boycotted and that no fair be held. On the night before the date that the fair should be held a

150

merchant in the town, one Eugene McCrohan, discussed the matter with some of his merchant colleagues on the point that if they did not hold a fair of some sort would they lose their moral claim to their rights to the fair. After much thought had been given they drew up a plan, secret to themselves, that they would hold a fair if only one single sale took place and thereby ensuring that in the event of any legal tangle they could truly say that a fair without tolls had been held.

About one minute past midnight on the morning of the day the fair should be held five of them went down a laneway in the town

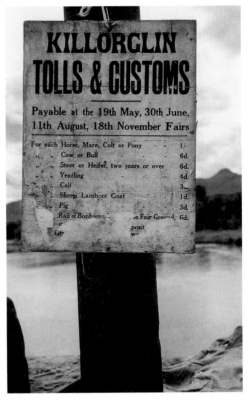

Tolls due at the fair, 1954. (Inge Morath © The Inge Morath Foundation. Courtesy of Magnum Photos)

to the cabin of a man who was known as 'Paddy The Goats'. Getting Paddy out of bed they asked him to get one of his goats from his herd and to come to the town square with them. Paddy readily agreed and they all went to the centre of the town. On arrival there Eugene McCrohan asked Paddy to sell the animal to a fellow merchant, to which Paddy readily agreed. The cash and the animal – a goat – changed hands and a transaction had taken place.[20]

The old custom had been broken and a new one established, and as a goat had been central in the victory, the animal then became a central feature of every fair held afterwards. However, as tolls were collected throughout the nineteenth century and until the 1960s, it is hard to imagine when a breaking of the custom took place.

Conclusion

The origin stories offered during the second half of the twentieth century vary as much as those of earlier years. The only theme which continued was that the goat was a symbol of the fair.

This idea may lie at the heart of the mystery of the origin of the goat ritual, although in a much more banal fashion: when the Foleys took over the running of the fair, they used a goat as a mascot for the fair, or for their faction. As time passed its simple origin was forgotten, or it ceased to be remarked upon. In later years, in response to intrusive questions from curious strangers, a series of explanations may have been presented to explain it, or to spice up its history. The familiar figures of Daniel O'Connell, Cromwell and St Patrick, all familiar elements of folk tradition, or major episodes from local history, such as the Tithe War, were drawn upon to provide explanations for the display.

Notes

1   A curse.
2   'May God be with all of you to the west'.
3   Liam Foley, 'Puck – The Mardi Gras of the South', *Kerryman*, 8 August 1945.
4   M.A. Murray, 'The Puck Fair of Killorglin', in *Folklore* 64, 1953, pages 351-354.
5   Kieran Foley, *History of Killorglin* (1988) page 3.
6   T.J. Barrington, *Discovering Kerry* (Blackwater Press, Dublin, 1976) page 41.
7   Kieran Foley, *History of Killorglin* (1988) page 3.
8   J.P. O'Sullivan, 'The Beauty of Puck Fair', *Kerry Champion*, 11 August 1951.
9   The text is reproduced as 'Puck Fair – Killorglin Ireland's Oldest Fair and Carnival' in Paddy MacMonagle, *Paddy Mac's Shreds & Patches* (Mac Publications, Killarney, 2010) pages 188-191.
10 Máire MacNeill, *The Festival of Lughnasa* (Oxford University Press, 1962) page 294.
11 'At the Fair of Puck', *Kerry Reporter*, 18 August 1928; 'Puck Fair', *Kerryman*, 15 August 1931.
12 Robert Gibbings, *Sweet Cork of Thee* (Dent, London, 1951) page 205.
13 Máire MacNeill, *The Festival of Lughnasa* (Oxford University Press, 1962) page 292.
14 Anthony M McCormack, *The Earldom of Desmond 1463-1583* (Four Courts Press, Dublin, 2005) page 29.
15 Patrick Logan, *Fair Day: The Story of Irish Fairs and Markets* (Appletree Press, Belfast, 1986) page 21.
16 Keith Alan Waters, *The Earls of Desmond in the Fourteenth Century*. Doctoral Thesis, Durham University (2004). Available at Durham E-Theses Online: http://etheses.dur.ac.uk/2818/
17 'Item 16, "Profits of the fair in Anye"', *The Peyton and Desmond Surveys. The Desmond Survey, Corpus of Electronic Texts Edition*, John A. Murphy, Electronic

edition compiled by Emer Purcell, 2009. A project of University College Cork, College Road, Cork, Ireland: http://www.ucc.ie/celt.

18 Patrick J. O'Connor, *Fairs and Markets of Ireland A Cultural Geography* (Oireacht na Mumhan Books, Newcastle West, 2003) page 24.

19 'Desmond Survey', *Kerryman*, 17 September 1927. The *Kerryman* reproduced parts of the Desmond Survey relating to County Kerry in a series of extracts published between 13 August and 15 October 1927.

20 Paddy O'Sullivan, 'How a Goat Saved a Fair', *Kerryman*, 5 August 1977.

Appendix III

Report of the Fair from the *Cork Examiner*, 1846[1]

TRALEE, WEDNESDAY. The anniversary of this ancient and remarkable fair was held yesterday, at Killorglin, as usual. This distinguishing appellation has been conferred on it from its being a great mart for goats – pucks – among the rest, at this season of the year; and, in order to pay a marked tribute of respect to that hardy race, a fatherly, sage looking mountain chieftain, antlered and bearded, is selected and adorned with the most grotesque finery. His body to the haunches is enveloped in folds of wreathed rushes – his head and horns embroidered with gilded gingerbread, and showy coloured ribbons, a fold of which passes along the back, and is allowed to be sufficiently lengthy to be used as reins. Sometimes heads of the salmon – a fish which abounds in the silvan rivers of this interesting locality, are placed on the hero's back, shaped in like a sidesaddle, and intended it is said, for the first farmer[']s daughter, who 'went out' – was married – as an encouragement to future aspirants. Thus caparisoned, the Lord of the Glencar mountains is led forth, amidst the shouts of the light-hearted mountaineers, through the oblong village and its dingy environs, followed by all the gypsies, tinkers, pedlars, pickpockets, and such characters, who are most regular frequenters of this frolicsome fair.

When the 'Foulowos' and the 'Pallatines' waged fierce and irreconcilable war, this was the arena in which a campaign would be commenced, or a pitched battle determined, and the party most eager for the fray, and most sanguine of success, made 'Puck' a signal of defiance, and over his devoted head, was the battle waged with barbarous impetuosity.

It is said that the ancient custom, which was at one time sacrilege, or cowardice to neglect, has now so far degenerated, that the outlawed animal is only beautified in his temporary regalities, when 'Big Mick', to whom the hereditary revenue of the fair belongs, has got a caubeen full of half crowns for custom. Then the peasantry, over whom he is considered a sort of Kaiser, lead forth the emblem of former but almost forgotten feudalism.

I regret to state, that this fair has been disturbed by a renewal of those foolish faction fights, which the clemency of the Assistant Barrister, at the last sessions, towards those who were brought before him, for similar offences, ought to have had a great effect in discountenancing. It was so desperately ferocious that the police force available did not think it prudent, as I am informed, to interfere.

Prices for milch cattle, store pigs, lambs, and sheep, were good, but not quite so high, as at the other late fairs.

Ponies, for which the fair is almost as celebrated as 'pucks', were there in multitudes, and many exchanged their rugged, healthy pastures for the productive demesnes of Leinster gentlemen.

The blind, halt, lean, galled jades[2] of drunken, trucking tinkers, with pedlars' mules and turners' jackasses, formed a fair proportion of the moving material of this well-known fair.

Notes
1 'Puck Fair', *Cork Examiner*, 17 August 1846. This forms the earliest detailed report of the fair.
2 'blind, halt, lean, galled jades': blind, lame, thin worthless nags, afflicted with saddle sores.

SELECT BIBLIOGRAPHY

NEWSPAPERS

Kerry Advocate, 1914-1915
Kerry Evening Post, 1828-1842
Kerry Examiner, 1840-1853
Kerry Independent, 1881-1883
Kerry Reporter, 1924-1935
Kerry Sentinel, 1878-1918
Kerryman, 1904-2012
Tralee Chronicle, 1843-1881
Tralee Mercury, 1833-1838

BOOK SECTIONS AND MAGAZINE ARTICLES

'The Billy-Goat of Puck Fair', *Strand Magazine*, Vol. 19, May 1900.
'Life Goes to an Irish Party', *LIFE*, 29 September 1941.
'Killorglin', in *Kerry County Guide and Maps*, 1964.
'Flashback. Puck of the Irish', *National Geographic Magazine*, Vol. 209, Issue 3, March 2006.
M.C.K., 'Puck Fair', *The Irish Monthly*, Vol. 22, July 1894.
S.M., 'Puck Fair', *Kerry Archaeological Magazine*, Vol. V, July 1919.
Foley, Kieran, 'Puck Fair, Killorglin', in *The Iveragh Peninsula: A Cultural Atlas of the Ring of Kerry* ed. John Crowley and John Sheehan (Cork University Press, Cork, 2009).
Gallop, Rodney, 'Puck Fair at Killorglin', *Geographical Magazine*, August 1942.
McNulty, Kieran, 'Revolutionary Movements in Kerry 1913 to 1923', *Journal of the Kerry Archaeological and Historical Society*, Series 2, Vol. 1, 2001.
Moraghan, Seán, 'Puck Fair in Cinema and Television', *The Kerry Magazine*, Issue 23, 2013.

Morris, Michael P., 'Puck Fair – Killorglin Ireland's Oldest Fair and Carnival', in Paddy MacMonagle, *Paddy Mac's Shreds & Patches* (Mac Publications, Killarney, 2010).

Munnelly, Tom, 'The Singing Tradition of Irish Travellers', *Folk Music Journal*, Vol. 3, Issues 1-2, 1975.

Murray, M.A., 'The Puck Fair of Killorglin', *Folklore* 64, 1953.

Proudfoot, Lindsay, 'Markets, Fairs and Towns in Ireland, *c*.1600-1853' in *Provincial Towns in Early Modern England and Ireland: Change, Convergence and Divergence* ed. Peter Borsay, Lindsay Proudfoot (Oxford University Press, Oxford, 2002).

Sheats, Dorothea, 'I Walked Some Irish Miles', *National Geographic Magazine*, Vol. 99, Issue 5, May 1951.

Walsh, Anthony, 'The Origin of Puck Fair', in *The Irishman's Annual* (Michael Glazier, Tralee, 1955).

Books

Barrington, T.J., *Discovering Kerry* (Blackwater Press, Dublin, 1976).

Bary, Valerie, *Houses of Kerry* (Ballinakella Press, County Clare, 1994).

Bell, Jonathan, and Mervyn Watson, *A History of Irish Farming 1750-1950* (Four Courts Press, Dublin, 2008).

Breathnach, Ciaran, and Aoife Bhreatnach, *Portraying Irish Travellers: Histories and Representations* (Cambridge Scholars Press, Newcastle, 2006).

Cronin, Denis A, *et al*, *Irish Fairs and Markets: Studies in Local History* (Four Courts Press, Dublin, 2001).

Foley, Kieran, *History of Killorglin* (1988).

Gibbings, Robert, *Sweet Cork of Thee* (Dent, London, 1951).

Gordon, Lady Edith Susan Leeson-Marshall, *The Winds of Time* (John Murray, London, 1934).

Hayward, Richard, *In the Kingdom of Kerry* (Dundalgan Press, Dundalk, 1946).

Hogg, Garry, *Turf Beneath My Feet* (Museum Press, London, 1950).

Houlihan, Michael, *Puck Fair History and Traditions* (Treaty Press, Limerick, 1999).

Houlihan, Patrick, *Cast a Laune Shadow: Reminiscences of Life in Killorglin* (1997).

Hussey, S.M., *Reminiscences of an Irish Land Agent* (Duckworth, London, 1904).

Johnson, Stowers, *Before and After Puck* (Fortune Press, London, 1953).

King, Noel, *Lifetimes – Folklore from Kerry* (Doghouse Books, Tralee, 2007).

Lever, Christopher, *The Naturalized Animals of the British Isles* (Hutchinson, London, 1977).

Lewis, Samuel, *A Topographical Dictionary of Ireland* Vol II (S Lewis & Co, London, 1837).

Logan, Patrick, *Fair Day: The Story of Irish Fairs and Markets* (Appletree Press, Belfast, 1986).

Lucey, Donnacha Seán, *Land, Popular Politics and Agrarian Violence in Ireland: The Case of County Kerry, 1872-86* (University College Dublin Press, Dublin, 2011).

Lynd, Robert, *Rambles in Ireland* (Mills and Boon, London, 1912).

McCormack, Anthony M., *The Earldom of Desmond 1463-1583: The Decline and Crisis of a Feudal Lordship* (Four Courts Press, Dublin, 2005).

MacNeill, Máire, *The Festival of Lughnasa* (Oxford University Press, 1962).

O'Carroll, Gerald, *The Pocket History of Kerry* (Polymath Press, Tralee, 2007).

O'Connor, Patrick J., *Fairs and Markets of Ireland A Cultural Geography* (Oireacht na Mumhan Books, Newcastle West, 2003).

O'Faolain, Seán, *An Irish Journey* (Longmans, London, 1940).

Rukeyser, Muriel, *The Orgy* (Andre Deutsch, London, 1965).

Smith, Charles, *The Ancient and Present State of the County of Kerry: A New Reader's Edition*, ed. Seán Moraghan (Bona Books, Killorglin, 2010).

Starkie, Walter, *Scholars and Gypsies* (John Murray, London, 1963).

Synge, J.M., *In Wicklow, West Kerry and Connemara* (Maunsell, Dublin, 1911).

_____, *In Wicklow, West Kerry and Connemara. Essays by George Gmelch and Ann Saddlemyer* (O'Brien Press, Dublin, 1980).

Thomas, Caitlin, *My Life With Dylan Thomas: Double Drink Story* (Virago, London, 2008).

Zuelow, Eric G.E., *Making Ireland Irish: Tourism and National Identity Since the Irish Civil War* (Syracuse University Press, New York, 2009).

PARLIAMENTARY PAPERS

'Report of the Commissioners Appointed to Inquire into the State of the Fairs and Markets in Ireland', in *Parliamentary Papers Vol. XLI, 1852-3* (HMSO, 1853).

THESIS

Waters, Keith Alan (2004) The Earls of Desmond in the Fourteenth Century. Doctoral Thesis, Durham University (2004). Available at Durham E-Theses Online: http://etheses.dur.ac.uk/2818/

FILMS

'Puck Fair' is Held in County Kerry. British Movietone News, 1933.

Puck Fair at Killorglin. British Movietone News, 1935.

Travellers Must Camp Outside Town. RTÉ Television, 1965

Puck Fair. RTÉ Television, 1965.

INTERNET SOURCES

www.books.google.com

www.britishnewspaperarchive.co.uk

www.irishnewsarchive.com

www.irishtimes.com/archive/

www.thepeerage.com

About the Author

Seán Moraghan previously edited Charles Smith's *The Ancient and Present State of the County of Kerry: A New Reader's Edition* (Bona Books, 2010). He has also published a number of articles about Kerry local history. He has worked as a librarian, bookseller, book indexer, tour guide, and folklore researcher.

If you enjoyed this book, you may also be interested in ...

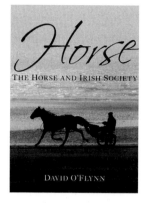

Horse: The Horse & Irish Society
DAVID O'FLYNN

Throughout the ages the horse has played a pivotal role in Irish society. It is a ubiquitous symbol in Ireland, present in many classic depictions of our culture, from loyal work horse to traditional horse fairs. Over a twelve-month period, David O'Flynn has collected a varied selection of images of the Irish horse, in these and other less clichéd guises, and discusses how the horse's role has mirrored the change in Irish culture as Ireland developed into a modern society.

978 1 84588 706 3

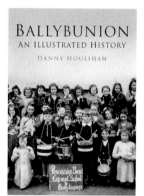

Ballybunion: An Illustrated History
DANNY HOULIHAN

Ballybunion: An Illustrated History, traces the history of the area from the arrival of the ancient shore dwellers along its coastline around 4000 BC through the Bronze Age, Iron Age and Early Christian settlements. The book takes the reader on a journey through the dawn of the medieval period, through the stories of fierce faction fights and the ghost ships which sailed the Shannon.

978 1 84588 999 9

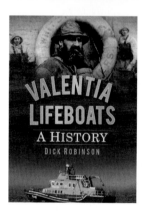

Valentia Lifeboats: A History
DICK ROBINSON

The lifeboats of Valentia have been in service since 1946. In this detailed history, Dick Robinson captures the spirit of the station, together with the tragedies and sacrifices that make up its history. It has been compiled using the first-hand accounts, original and rare images, and detailed records of the station. It is a fitting tribute to the people who have served here, and will be a record of the station for many years to come.

978 1 84588 707 0

Visit our websites and discover thousands of other History Press books.

www.thehistorypress.ie
www.thehistorypress.co.uk

The History Press Ireland